THE
DEATH
OF OUR
DREAMS

AND OTHER FUNNY STORIES

A.J. SCHMITZ

MAXIXAM
PRESS

For Caroline and Jim.

I've crunched the numbers and I believe
we are worth more alive than dead.

Everything in this book is true.

Some of the names have been changed
to protect the guilty and because I couldn't
remember their actual names.

CONTENTS

THE DOWNSIDE OF SELF-PUBLISHING 1

GRASP MY HALLUX 13

MONEY, MONEY, MONEY 25

BOMBA THE BULLSHIT ARTIST 35

CROSSTOWN TRAFFIC 55

PASSWORDZ_33!$ 65

AXE MUDERER INN 75

HOL-I-DAY EQUAL-I-TAY 101

GOVERMENT CHEESE 109

NIGHT WIGGA 119

TEETH, TATTOOS AND TOES 153

I HATE A PARADE 171

WHITE COLLAR WORKER 181

THE BAUBLE GAUNTLET 197

NEW YORK ART SCENE 205

THE GOODALLS 219

THE DEATH OF OUR DREAMS 229

THE DOWNSIDE
OF SELF-PUBLISHING

In the introduction of my first book *Buggin' Out*, I stated some solid reasons why it was my desire to self-publish my own book.

Besides a fear of drug-induced anal rape, which I realize now is not what happens to most people during the publishing process, I simply didn't want to go through the exhausting routine of trying to get an agent to read my book. It's an incredibly labor-intensive process that can take months, if not *years* of work and pumps heaping doses of rejection into your veins until you question your very existence on earth.

Trying to find an agent is a soul-stabbing task, but it also takes precious time away from what I really want to do in the first place, which is write.

Writing query letters doesn't count. Writing query letters to agents I researched online so I can pretend they're the perfect person to handle my juicy material is a bullshit muscle that even I, an expert bullshitter, is incapable of flexing. These query letters have the same ring to them as cover letters I've sent to job postings.

"Oh, yes, I'd love to be an assistant manager in your warehouse because it's my dream to give 50 hours of my life each week to your company for shit wages so I can live paycheck-to-paycheck. When I was bouncing on my grandfather's knee, he asked me what I wanted to be when I grew up and of course I told him it was to be an assistant manager at your warehouse, overseeing a collection of cutthroat scabs who'd gut me from chin to crotch the second my head was turned so they can eat the tuna sandwich I left in the fridge. I hope you will consider me for the job. Attached is my resume, which is a timeline of over-glorified tasks I've done for other soulless companies that barely paid me a living wage."

I wasn't about to let a mousy bookworm who hasn't seen sunshine in three years . . . or a random incel slug who has never shared an 8-ball of cocaine with a hooker gate-keep my work.

I mean, who are these faceless agents determining whether my work can be on bookshelves or not?

I'm sure they're all fine, warm-hearted, college-educated people with everyday problems like loud neighbors, high medicine costs and crushing depression… but fuck them! My book is good enough to be out in the public -- stirring the hearts and minds of everyone who reads it. So I'll put it out there myself, thank you very much!

I eliminated the countless hours of research and writing agents so I could apply that energy to writing more books.

Like the one you're reading now!

The second reason I self-published *Buggin' Out* was because I wanted complete control of my work. I wanted to write it the way I wanted it, obviously, but I also wanted to design the book jacket, lay it out and have complete artistic freedom in every facet. I chose my editors and listened to their advice and the result was a book that was totally mine in every way. It was a wonderful creative achievement!

But, since I eliminated the agent portion of the process, what the hell else was I going to do? Of course I was going to design and lay it out myself. It's SELF-publishing. It was just me against the world and that was the terrible, lonely and misguided decision I had to live with.

Not only am I the writer and designer, I'm now the agent and the sole marketer! Which brings me to the third reason I self-published. Since I work in the field of adverting and marketing, I wanted to market *Buggin' Out*, thinking I'd be just as good, if not *better*, at marketing my own material than someone else. At least, that's the load of expert-level bullshit I told myself.

I claim to want to do more writing, but I take on the task of marketing and advertising, which is a job in itself. And I've never marketed a book before, so it's an unfamiliar field for me. As it turns out, it's more labor intensive than I thought. Between my *job* job, the book marketing job, writing, freelancing and being a father and a husband, I've whittled my free time down to about 15 minutes a day. I use those precious 15 minutes to grab a screwdriver and fix something in my house so it doesn't fall down and kill someone.

Here I am a writer -- self-publishing a book and marketing it and I'm telling myself that this is the way to go and totally believing it. The only way to get through the process is to give myself a split personality. A new guy to counteract the downtrodden guy who thinks nothing will work out.

The new guy is a dreamer and he can see the pot of gold at the end of the hard-work rainbow! The Optimist! The Pessimist is persistent and negative. The Optimist has fire in his soul. The Optimist also drinks a fair amount of wine, so he can get belligerent and can actually bully the Pessimist, which is not a pretty sight. Especially when all the bickering spills out of my brain and into the real world. My wife steps out of the shower and asks me if I heard voices and I wrinkle my brow like she's some kind of idiot, but then I realize the argument between the Pessimist and the Optimist in my *brain* was actually happening out loud in the kitchen. If I'm not careful, large men in white coats will knock on my door and I'll have to do my writing in a padded room with crayons, which, the more I think about, the more I find very pleasing... which is a very dangerous thought process to have!

So, how did I approach the whole self-publishing thing?

Well, after all the brilliant writing, phenomenal layout and dazzling cover designing... I upload it to Amazon, which we all know, is a glorious and fair company that is absolutely NOT a monopoly. I've been using Amazon for about 25 years and I love it. So do you. Don't tell me you don't, because that's bullshit and as I said before, I'm an expert in the field of bullshit. All is good. I fix a few spelling mistakes, tighten things up and release the book to absolutely no fanfare whatsoever. I tell almost no one except my sister and my buddy Ian.

I post the announcement of the book's release on social media and everyone is like "What the hell, you wrote a book? Congrats!"

Even my mom was like "You wrote a book, mister? When were you going to tell us, the people who *raised* you?" That message came in a text message and was accompanied by an angry-face emoji, which really cut to my soul. Damn emojis!

Very effective those little faces!

I sell some books to family and friends and it's well-received. Are they being polite or is it genuine praise? I don't know. I think the book is excellent. They think it's excellent. But maybe they're being polite. Maybe they think it sucks. I suddenly get a third personality... Paranoid Guy. This psycho can't be bullied or talked to by either of the original duo of the Pessimist and Optimist, so there's no choice but to introduce a fourth personality... Bartender. This guy takes care of everyone equally, but he gets out of control and he hires a Therapist. Now my daily routine is five guys screaming at each other in my head. Forget about the REAL me -- the writer/artist guy. He's in a lounge chair with a bag of popcorn watching this mess from the balcony.

Of course being the professional Marketer that I am, I do market research for the book. I'm wondering when to post to Twitter, and Facebook. I design a complete campaign, which I'll pay to push on social media. But first I need to check a few boxes. First and foremost, I need to get Amazon reviews. Easy, right? Hell no! Your friends and family are more than happy to give you a big fat congrats on Facebook… they'll even give you that little horn and confetti emoji that is super cute and celebratory. But get them to give you an Amazon review? Might as well try and yank the fang out of a lion's mouth while wearing a crown of prime pork chops. It's impossible… and you can only ask for an Amazon review so many times before you come across as a desperate jerk who does nothing but market to his loyal friends and family, who, by the way, are also running around like maniacs with screwdrivers trying to prevent their house from crushing their loved ones because they only have 15 minutes of free time.

Eventually I gave up trying to get Amazon reviews and launched the campaign. I spend actual money… money my sister lent me because she's awesome and believes in my talent. She wanted to help, so I take this precious money and throw it at a campaign. I go to the twisted and fractured society known as "the internet" and start feeding the beast actual hard-earned cash. For all I know, the money is going directly into the bank account of some blood-sucking corporate vampire who needs a new Lamborghini like a hole in the fucking head. But I feed the beast anyway.

I've also chosen to market at a slow time of the year… March… at the "tail-end" of the COVID-19 pandemic… while Vladimir Putin, affectionately known as Hitler II,

AND OTHER FUNNY STORIES

is trying to start World War III. Gas prices are at an all-time high, and everyone is on the brink of going insane, but sure… why not try to sell some books?

Everyone needs something to read on the beach, yeah? The warm weather is coming and if we're not getting our skins fried off by nuclear bombs, we can fry our skins off with the sun's deadly rays. Let's pair that with a good book, shall we? My book!

I mix my magical elixir of design, messaging and stupidity and launch a Facebook campaign. I start on March 16 -- the day after the Ides of March because I fear that on some level, I may get stabbed in the back like Julius Caesar. It launches on Wednesday. I target the UK, Canada and the United States. English speaking places that may enjoy my snarky, miserable attitude and have a few laughs.

It gets some looks and some traction, but only a few clicks, so I decide to crank the knob on the budget dial from $35 to a whopping $140 for Thursday. That's also St. Patrick's Day and I figured I might get a few drunken purchases or so. My wife loves to go to the mall with me after I've had a cocktail or two because I tend to let my guard down. She jams a fashionable handbag in my face and says, "This is nice! Don't you think this is nice?" Then she's twirling in front of a full-length mirror and posing, which is shocking because we're standing in line to get a pretzel. Somehow, my wife always finds something to buy regardless of our location. I could be at the McDonald's drive through and turn to see my wife modeling shoes… "These are nice! Don't you think these are nice?"

The higher Facebook campaign budget obtains more engagement and gets more clicks. Not one, not two, but *three* people actually "like" my ad. One woman gives me a HEART! I won't complain about it, maybe it gets more eyes on the ad. Usually people who like ads on Facebook are some kind of Satan worshiper, but if they're clicking on *my* ad, well, these are fine upstanding citizens of the world! They know an independent writer is out there hustling for his art and they've chosen to help me with an uplifting heart.

While checking Facebook on my phone, I get an ad for *Buggin' Out* on my timeline. Now I'm paying to advertise to myself!

I decide to adjust where I'm advertising. I get 17,000 looks in the United Kingdom, but no clicks, so I eliminate the UK completely. Do people in the UK even laugh? I can't think of anything funny to come out of the UK since Monty Python, so I cut them out. Then I ponder eliminating some age ranges. 18-25? No, that age range can enjoy the book. What about 65+? I can't cut them. A good chunk of the people that have praised the book are above 65, so I keep them.

Finally, after five long days... of watching the engagement totals... of refreshing the Facebook Ad dashboard and looking at the Amazon totals report... my $400 and five days of constant worry has netted me... drum roll please... four sales. FOUR! That's $100 a book.

I default to what I always do in these situations: stare out at some distant trees and wonder how long it would take to build a log cabin. Then I wonder if I can survive in the log cabin because I've grown soft and dependable on the tit of our modern world. Sure, living in a log cabin seems great… clean air, dirty living. Then I'll run out of coffee and I'll panic. I'll need to go into town and interact with people. Kids will halt their bikes on the sidewalk and stare at me as I enter the general store. They'll point and whisper, "Isn't that crazy A.J.? The old man that lives in the cabin at the foot of the hills?" Kids don't whisper well… most kids don't learn the art of whispering till they're older, so I'll hear them as I yank the rusty screen door open and step foot inside the general store. I'll turn and give the kids a morbid glance and belch -- my only response to anything at that point. The kids will shudder and peel off. I'll collect my coffee, maybe a newspaper to re-connect me to the civilized world. I'll toss some rumpled bills onto the counter and walk off without a word.

Then I realize I'm over reacting to the whole Facebook campaign and I get back on the horse… or, behind the computer… and start a Twitter campaign. I won't bore you with the intricate details, but guess how many sales this advertising juggernaut mustered? Two. Two fucking books!! I spend $300 and sold two books. My return on investment got worse. That's $150 a book!

After I spend a whopping $1,100 on an Amazon campaign to sell 32 books… that's $34 a book, I call it a day on paid *Buggin' Out* advertising.

My last vestige of hope is a book signing and chat that I've scheduled at a bookstore on the north shore of Long Island -- The Dolphin Bookshop in Port Washington. After I contacted every bookstore on Long Island to set up a rousing tour of signings from Garden City to Montauk, I was met with two responses. One of them was a place that was out of business. The other was The Dolphin Bookshop.

Robin at Dolphin sets up the event after reading my book and is super nice and enthusiastic about the signing. I call a few days before the 'Meet The Author' event to see if everything is good to go and if I need to bring anything... like tequila or anti-depressants. Barbara, who answers the phone, informs me with a ring in her voice like wedding bells that "Robin has left the country!"

Left the country?!

That gleeful bit of news hits me on the head like a watermelon. It does NOT instill confidence. I'd been confiding in Robin the whole time, but I suppose she saw the writing on the wall... the signing was going to be a shit show and she not only bailed... she left the continent!

Again, social media is used to paper the world with the announcement of my signing. A few professional emails are sent as well. Dolphin sends some eblasts about the event and I was featured in a free Long Island activities paper called *Good Times*.

Guess how many people came to this shindig? Four people. FOUR! And one of them was my father and he was exhausted because he ate too much chocolate cake the night before and had a bad night's sleep.

I fire everyone in my head. Optimist, Pessimist... Drunks... all of them! At this point, I'm completely done with *Buggin' Out*. I'm done talking about it, advertising it... I don't even want to look at it anymore. It's like when a couple decides their firstborn child isn't worth saving anymore and focuses their attention on kid number two. The first child will become something terribly embarrassing -- like a porn star -- and the second child will become a scientist that cures Athlete's Foot.

Child two is this book you're holding. I'm positive this book is what rockets me to stardom and gives me the desired fortune I need to do all the things in life I want to do. Like buy some sneakers that are not in the sales rack, or perhaps, fill the gas tank of my car so I can drive and eat in a restaurant by the shore.

Enjoy.

THE DEATH OF OUR DREAMS

GRASP MY HALLUX

Years ago, I worked with a guy named Ed and he was the second youngest of 23 children. 23 children! When he was 50, his oldest sister was 84. What's shocking is the fact that Ed's mother had another human being inside her body for half her adult life. His parents obviously didn't believe in birth control. Did either of them ever say, "this is freakin' nuts, we have to stop?" Was there a marker? Baby 12… 19? I mean 23 children isn't a family; it's an army battalion. Someone must have gone hungry in that clan. Let's say Ed's mother got pregnant at 15 and had her first child just after she turned 16. That means she had children until she was 51 years old. Most women have trouble giving birth after the age of 40. It's a stunning accomplishment. I'm sure someone tried to shake her hand at the achievement, but she couldn't reciprocate because she had an arm-full of babies.

I believe when people are banging out 23 kids, it's about religion and the denouncement of birth control. But perhaps it's about a fear of the family name dying out and spreading one's seed… something of that nature. I have one kid and I'm pretty exhausted all the time, so 23 children seems inconceivable to me. But I believe once you reach kid number five, they start taking care of each other in a pecking order arrangement.

My son Max is writing a book on anthropology. Like doing actual research: drawing skulls and tracking how certain subhuman species died off while others lived on and creating tracking maps.

It's fascinating stuff. He's 11. He tells me about his findings over waffles at breakfast. He's writing a dissertation about human beings and the beginning of intelligent life and I stare out the window and wonder why at the end of *Star Wars: Revenge of the Sith*, Darth Vader had a fully formed Darth Vader outfit already. I mean, was the whole outfit ready to go right off the rack? Who designed the outfit? Did they have fashion designers? I would have thought after Obi Wan Kenobi lopped Anakin Skywalker's legs off, The Emperor would have stuck poor 'Ani' into an iron lung, or something that resembled a diving bell. Then Darth would piece his ensemble together as time went on. Maybe a cape here… a belt with blinking lights there… but no -- instant Darth Vader outfit!

"Papa, did you know it's pronounced Neander-TALL and not Neander-TH-all?"

This amazing announcement brings me back down to earth and into the kitchen again. "Really?" I ask.

"Yea," He nods.

And just like that, another of life's seemingly familiar lexicons is shattered into pieces. We've been saying Neanderthal wrong all this time? No one bothered to correct us? Oh well. It's just a thing I guess. Like the way we call the big city in France, Par-IS, and the French call it, Par-EE. I will continue to call it Paris and call the hunched over monkey men NeanderTHALLs, because my tongue won't do it any other way.

More shocking than the Neanderthal pronunciation is when Max told me dinosaurs and humans didn't live together. When I was a kid, the Saturday morning cartoons depicted cavemen riding dinosaurs like horses and having all sorts of whacky adventures. Surely Hanna Barbera knew a thing or two about the history of man... but nope. All wrong. Those cartoons would also show a caveman knocking a cavewoman over the skull with a club and dragging her by the hair into a cave as a mating ritual... so perhaps I wasn't properly educated by these primitive animated shows at all.

Then Max continues his discourse on anthropology while licking peanut butter off his fingertips.

"Did you know that the Arthropithicus-blahblah-fripticus farmed and planted crops? Most people think they were just hunter/gatherers, but there's evidence that they planted and harvested crops and used farming tools."

"Wow," I say, "That's fascinating."

But then my mind begins to wander again. Not to the Star Wars universe, but to those charts. You've seen those charts before. A series of shadow figures -- man goes from some kind of legged fish, to knuckle dragging NeaderTHALL, to homo-erectus, to modern man and in some cases, to a fully evolved tennis player or a briefcase-toting business man. I suppose it's a statement about our hobbies or maybe our fate. I think if it we're to predict our actual future, man's final form would be some kind of blob with a giant cranium and an IV feeding tube going directly into the stomach.

Most humans are evolving. My son is somehow *devolving*. It's been said that sometimes a man makes an animal of himself to take away the pain of being human. Maybe that's true, but my son is devolving into an ape because apes seem to be having a marvelous time. Max hunches over... his arms an inch above the ground and bounces on the furniture like it's a jungle gym. He eats with his hands and smells everything like a dog. He's fascinated by how humans came to be. How we were all sorts of various ape-like humanoids who evolved and became the animals we are today. Some of these apes died off while others got through on jolly good spirits and the ability to survive eating wormy meats and rotting berries.

My wife on the other hand does not share this Darwinian philosophy. She was raised on a steady diet of The Holy Bible and anything my son says about ape-men is met with the steely glare of blasphemy. I get caught in the middle of the melee when all I want to do is pair an excellent wine with my rib eye steak... exactly how Jesus and the monkey-men wrote it in the Constitution.

Erroneous theology aside, I'm still surprised at my wife's dedication to The Bible. Not that religion as a principal guide should be a shock to anyone. Billions of people adhere to some kind of religious life path.

My shock stems from my belief that Rita is actually a monkey. We got her one of those *23 and Me* tests and there was no signs of monkey in there. It actually revealed her to be a nice mash-up of Native American and Portuguese. Still, I was perplexed to find no revelation of orangutan or baboon in Rita's test. This isn't an insult. It's a fact. If you're not careful, my wife will curl up behind you and take a dominating position over the top of your head and pick through your hair like a chimpanzee. She'll have your shaggy mane standing on end like you stuck your finger in a light socket. She'll sift through each stand of hair -- as if a note from school was received about a head lice infestation. Rita picks, sifts, scratches and combs over our skulls with the precision of a gorilla queen with perfectly manicured nails. Max and I walk around with perpetual bed head. He and I could easily start a New Wave band called *A Flock of Rhesus*. All we need to complete the look is sunglasses and keytars.

Rita does stop short of eating the things she finds in our hair though. Monkeys tend to nibble on these findings, as they can be short on food supplies in the jungle. Rita is well fed. We put food in her cage. I'm kidding! ...she sleeps in a bed like you and me. Rita usually tosses whatever dandruff and flake pieces she discovers in our hair into the air, which usually falls into our faces. But the evidence of her monkey-ness doesn't fall primarily with the hair-picking thing. Rita kind of *looks* like a monkey. Again, not really an insult as I'm attracted to monkey-looking women. Maybe it is an insult... I don't know. But she's super hot! ...in a monkey way.

Listen, everyone has their flavor... chocolate, vanilla.... tall blondes... petite monkey women...

Strangely enough, Rita also kind of looks like an owl. It's possible one of her ancestors was an owl that mated with some species of spider monkey. But there was no owl DNA in the *23 and Me* test either, so that theory goes out the window too.

Perhaps the meeting of the owl and the monkey happened on Noah's Ark. It's possible! When people (and animals I suppose) are paired and forced into close quarters, strange things happen. Eyes begin to wander -- whether the eyes are forward facing or on the sides of the head -- they can wander. While the earth was flooded, maybe some of those monkey people that scientists are searching for got washed into oblivion... like the Missing Link. The Missing Link is the elusive 'evolution puzzle piece' that we keep hunting for and hope to stick into its glaring empty space and propel the scientific community to shout EUREKA! A lock that snaps in place and chains it all together – connecting the apes to the humans with a resounding YES! An answer to all our questions as to how we got here and why.

I'm not sure how we all got here and I'm not sure I care why. My theory is it has something to do with our thumbs. They slid up next to our other fingers and it gave us the amazing ability to swing a stick, twist a screwdriver or handle an Uzi. But it also gave us the amazing ability to use a typewriter or smash the button of a nuclear weapon. The thumb may be the most dangerous weapon ever invented! It has flattened cities and wiped out civilizations. The thumb is the basis of our corporate world as we know it. It fires the furnaces of capitalism. It holds the clipboard and it's used to give a hearty 'thumbs down' when the profit slips into the red. We need to blame the dire problems on someone and the thumb can also point at the guy who should be tossed into the furnace. In a company's desperate attempt to save money, they'll eliminate a person who they think is expendable. A big cheese boss tells one of his lackey yes-men, "save some money," and that's exactly what that lackey does. Even if in the long run it kills the workflow and identity of what was working so well in the first place. Sort of like a surgeon deciding—without any research, future speculation or thought to alternative options at all—to cut off the thumb to save the hand. The hand is saved, sure, but the hand is now completely non-functional.

The company tries to fix the problem by replacing the thumb. "why don't we stick a metal thumb on there as a replacement... or perhaps a fresh toe?" It will be glued, sewn on or perhaps carelessly tossed into place, but it doesn't compare with the former fully-functioning original, and again the hand will be virtually worthless. Now the real thumb is gone, an imposter is in its place and it's not possible to put the old thumb back—the surgery for that type of procedure hasn't been invented yet. You know what the company will do to fix this particular problem? Throw money at it. In fact, the money that was initially saved when cutting the original thumb probably has to be used to fix this mess. Now, some other poor bastard in the company with a sick child and overdue credit card bills will probably be kicked to the curb in an effort to save the company the cash they wanted to save in the first thumb-chopping incident. It's a vicious cycle. Darth Vader was pieced together like this and look how he turned out!

Don't let any of these balding billionaires with their fancy cars and hair plugs give you a false sense to the real nature of their corporate head-honcho vampirism. These savages will grind you, and those you love, into hamburger and happily serve it up at their next backyard bar-b-que in the Hamptons. In fact, they'll give the recipe to their friends and laugh about it as they drink your blood from fine crystal goblets.

These guys are real life Darth Vaders! They're one step away from becoming a James Bond villain. They've added rocket fuel to the fire of a new and exciting space race. Space is free and if they can get up there and back again, they go for it. And they have. The Earth is crowded and there's lots of room for expansion on Mars and the Moon. There's prime real estate for billboards and colonization.

I can barely afford my rent but the moon is secretly being divided up into little pie slices, none of which I'll ever have. We've just reached the 8-billion persons mark on this planet, yet the richest people are becoming more entitled to the point that they're approaching royalty in their mannerisms and thinking. With their noses held high, they step off their tax-free private jets, paid in full off the misery of the common worker, believing their riches were self-made.

This is the type of attitude that causes the masses to start rioting and if people don't watch their backs, heads will start to roll...

"Or at least a few thumbs may drop," I shout, banging the table, as I conclude my rant.

Max is shaking his head.

"What?" I ask.

This all seems philosophically sound to me, but Max, the professor, says it's all wrong and that the thumb means nothing in evolution. I feel like I just got demoted to middle manager! He says if anything, it's all about the Grasping Hallux. At one point, us monkey people had a toe that stuck out like a thumb and we could use it like a hand. I think to myself, "that's all fine for hanging upside down but it surely doesn't help climb the corporate ladder!" By the time I'm ready to express that sentiment, he's talking about how our preconceived notions about prehistoric man's life are all wrong as well. They could sew and all sorts of other crap.

"Sew?" I say in genuine shock.

"Yea," Max confirms.

Now I'm convinced that Neanderthals had fashion shows and runway models with judges. They turned those thumbs up by judging the artistry of newly sewn tiger capes or approved the sexiest crescent-shaped forehead on a fellow Homo Habilis. They had the Grasping Hallux, which gave them four hands essentially, each with the ability to turn a thumb down towards the center of the Earth. Four thumbs are much more effective than two. One person could essentially be a voting committee, giving four thumbs down, which propels the decision to fling a less evolved tribe-mate into the bonfire.

The breakfast lesson continues...

"Scientists found a finger or something in a cave... they called it Denisovan or something and it might be the closest thing they've found to humans."

The missing link?! I shout in my head.

"Some little girl found it in a cave while playing one day."

We have bands of scientists digging holes around the planet looking for artifacts and a little girl stumbles upon a finger and connects the Missing Link?! How appropriate. Max snatches my phone and shows me the archeological find. It's literally a knuckle. How anyone could decipher this little nub of chewy cartilage over a common piece of rubble that litters the entire planet is beyond me. But I suppose that's why they're scientists. They can see these things when I can't. I can tell the difference between a mint and near mint issue of Wolverine #1 in seconds while other are stumped. We all have our special gifts.

But how did a little girl discover the Denisovans? Is it a Latin word for devotion? What were they devoted to? Were they advanced enough to worship a god? Did they pray to an idol? Did they sew? Jesus H Christmas, no wonder Darth Vader had a fully formed Vader outfit! If monkey men can kneel before a fabricated god, sew clothing and have fashion shows, then surely the advanced world of Star Wars can slap together a fleshed-out Vader outfit in seconds.

We should be thankful we don't have four thumbs. If that were the case, we could have blown each other off the map decades ago. Another thumb creeping towards the button is enough to scare the hair off your back. If upper management could hold two or three more clipboards, they'd surely want you to work three times harder until you basically went sleepless... plowing like a zombie through your third job. They could hang you in a closet by your grasping hallux for a 15-minute power nap, but then you'd be expected to use your free thumbs to dial a phone or crank out an extra Darth Vader outfit.

"We're starting to learn about Mesopotamia and ancient Egypt in school," Max confesses. "You know what Mesopotamia is?"

I blink a few times and hold the warm coffee mug to my cheek.

"That's in like... the middle east or something. Right?"

This is an admission that I learned nothing in school, but Max takes it as a gentle softball pitch to whack out of the park. Before I know it, he's talking about the first civilizations and the wheel and crop-planting and languages.

Of course, my mind wanders to those monkey men. The scene in *2001: A Space Odyssey* where they touch the monolith and suddenly their brains cooled to the proper level of absorption and formed ideas. They use thighbones as weapons and drew penises on the cave wall. Soon, they're dancing around with golden King Tut hats and walking like an Egyptian. I realize quickly that we're monkeys as well -- sophisticated monkeys with modern problems. Modern questions. Like how will I afford my mud hut and how much will I get paid for my cave drawings?

MONEY, MONEY, MONEY

They say *money doesn't buy happiness* and that may be true, but it can definitely stave off misery. The person who originally wrote that absurd statement probably did so while navigating their 50-foot yacht into a Saint-Tropez docking bay. There's nothing rich folks like to give more than statements about how money isn't important. They chortle, "Money isn't important - family is" while being airlifted by helicopter with their family to a lush resort on the edge of a picturesque volcano. It's like when someone writes a book about how to make money and slaps a $50 price tag on it.

They also say that *money is the root of all evil* and I don't think that's true, but it's definitely the root of most household arguments. The person who made this factual claim must have done so at the peak of frustration. You don't claim that money is the root of all evil unless some fat cat is standing over your twisted torso, laughing maniacally while lighting a sycamore-sized cigar with a flaming hundred-dollar bill.

They also say that *money doesn't grow on trees* and that's very true because I've looked to trees in desperation. Where do you turn to when you need something so badly? The world of course! Money, heroin... friendship.

You think it's possible someone accidently dropped a roll of $100 bills under a random bush or lost a bag of China White in the oily gutter of the city. But you look around and all you see is the cold world of reality.

They tend to say a lot about money and I'm not sure who *they* are. Probably people with a lot of money... or people who want to hold onto their money. I don't talk about money because I have none. I talk about having no money, which is different than talking about money. Talking about the absence of money is to talk about desperation. It's about tough choices and being honest with what you want and what you need. Sometimes they're the same thing. Do I need food today? Are three meals totally necessary?

They say *don't spend your money before you've earned it*, and I know for a fact it's true. That's basically a rewording of *don't count your chickens before they hatch*. But spending money you don't have is the basis of our stupid credit system, so I don't know who actually came up with that statement. Probably someone NOT in the credit card business. Credit somehow became the gold standard in the world and I'm not sure why. It's basically a value system of future trust.

All I know is it's another thing I'll fail to do properly because I'm too busy working. I work and work, until I hear an email ping from a corporation that tells me my bill is past due. I have one of those credit monitoring services that tell me how my credit is doing. Every time I check it gives me a giant "meh." I filed for bankruptcy years ago and had to start rebuilding my credit, which means getting credit cards and buying stuff, which is the process that got me in hot water to begin with. My problems grew from hospital bills and not because I bought a 2011 Bugatti Veyron.

They say *don't spend all your money in one place* and that's easy enough to achieve, unless you go to the hospital… then you could potentially spend all your money plus all the money you plan to make in the future. Cancer or any other big health hurdle can wipe out your finances or put you in debt forever… without any way to climb out of the hole. It's frightening! It makes you think about life differently. One casual step off a curb or one clumsy yank of some gym equipment and you could cripple your bank account for a long, long time. If you're planning on buying a house, you'll definitely spend all your money in one place. Literally. The place you'll be living. A shit-box costs a million dollars these days.

Back in the 1950s, you could but a house, two cars, a dog and have endless stress-free bar-b-ques in the backyard of said house with the money you find under the sofa cushions. It was the American Dream. Now you'll be lucky to rent a shack in the woods for all your monthly paychecks, plus your soul. Even a new car can trickle your funds into one place. And if you're not careful, you could be living in your car, so make sure you get one that's comfortable and roomy. Perhaps that's why everyone drives SUVs now. As a safety net for when their home is suddenly on wheels.

They say *money is freedom* and that's true. Fuel costs money. If you step on the gas pedal of your car that has no gas in the tank, you don't get very far. Have you ever tried to go skiing with no money? They'll laugh you off the mountain.

Poor people don't travel. They stay where they are and are forced to judge the world from their bitter, manipulated point-of-view. Some people will say you can be free without money. That's called walking. Walking is great, until you need shoes, which cost money. If you walk, you'll eventually need to stop and rest. Most law enforcement agencies frown on people dropping and sleeping where they are. You could get a ticket, which costs money. Or you could choose to avoid that kind of disruption by getting a cheap motel, which costs money. The body only travels so far without fuel, so you'll need food, which costs money. Unless you grow your own, which seems hard to keep track of if you're walking somewhere else, so you'll need money. Don't let anyone tell you that you don't need money.

They say *you should invest your money wisely* and I do. In tequila. Not tequila stocks but in bottles. I drink it to forget I have no money and it works. Until the effects wear off and I feel like shit because I'm hungover and poor. I don't have any money to invest in stocks. The stock market confuses me as it does most human beings.

I worked on the commodities floor in New York City

for three months around Christmas of 2003. Two guys had a heart attack in that span. I figured at that rate, no one would be left, but there's always fresh meat to fill in the gaps. Someone comes along and starts screaming where the last screaming guy was standing. I was in the heating oil division. If you've never had the pleasure of being on a trading floor, consider yourself lucky. It's truly the worst place on the planet beside a concentration camp. I'm not sure why anyone would want to get into the business. Now it's all computers, but when I was there it was a bunch of guys standing in a circle and screaming at each other... and computers. I was a computer check clerk. I worked with a trader named John Devivo. John would join the pit of screamers and scream numbers and hold up complicated finger gestures until someone pointed at him and finger-gestured back. Then they'd scribble on paper, rip the paper in half and toss one half into a pit that they all were standing around. The paper would float down into an underground chamber, where it would be collected by packs of dark sub-humans dressed in black with bat wings and horns.

The underground dwellers would take the ticket that was tossed and enter it into the computer system...

Okay, maybe the demon pit thing was my imagination. My memory is fuzzy. Actually, John would tuck the other half of the ticket between his knuckles and continue to scream. My job was to literally jam my hand into the pack of bodies, feel around for John's hand and snatch his tickets. I'd take the tickets, run to my computer and cross-reference what the underground dwellers (fellow trader's computer clerk) had entered into the system based on John and the other trader's agreements. If the trade matched up, all good. If it didn't... I don't know what the hell we did. Threw a body into the underground pit? Does it matter?

It was a complete and utter shit-show on wheels. The only thing I can compare it to mentally is being in a gun battle. The amount of screaming and shouting was ludicrous, superseded in absurdity only by the number of phones some traders could place to their ear before they ran out of orifices to listen with.

Overhead, there was a massive, electronic board filled with green, yellow and red lights, with numbers and names, that resembled a spaceship and was probably the envy of every dictator who craved a giant board in their war room.

The board was blinking the names of the S&P 500 and Nasdaq companies and other terms I knew nothing about. At the end of the day, we'd all filter out together quietly. Kind of like pro wrestlers who'd beaten the living snot out of one another all day. At the beginning of the day, they talked cordially about what they were doing to each other...

"I'm going to do a flying elbow to the back of your ear," then walk to the arena and crush each other.

It was a bloody battle, but when the whistle blew, the crew calmly embraced one another and went to a bar where they'd drink like fish and talk about money.

They say *money can't buy you love* and that is absolutely true, but it can buy you companionship. Some of it can be rented by the hour or it can last a lifetime, depending on who's supplying the money and who's demanding it... and how long the lifetime is.

We've all seen the 28-year-old femme fatale who falls

madly in love with an 80-year-old geezer.

It's hard to resist an 80-year-old man in bed... his deathbed.

Sometimes, a few years of happiness is all some need. If you play your cards right, you can fall in love with that 28-year-old and start the vicious cycle all over again.

They say *money costs too much* and that is like... a play on words I believe, or a simile. Some will say it's irony. Most people will hear that statement and nod because it's true, but they don't know exactly why. They think about what money costs and realize it costs your soul and then dread hits them like a flying roundhouse kick to the face. Money costs time... time away from the things you love, time away from your family and time away from your dreams.

They say *money makes the world go around* and that is more about the economy than about science. The world spins just fine on its own without financial aid. It spins because it's a giant living ball, hurtling through space at 10,000 miles an hour, which makes perfect sense.

The economy makes no sense at all. I work hard and then I'm handed a paycheck, but there are others out there whose sole job it is to understand money and all it does. They're called *economists* and these savages are the reason you can't afford to do anything or go anywhere. A million years ago, when a caveman wanted a fish, he either got one or he took something that had value, like a fox pelt, and handed it over to the guy with the fish. Today, money is so complicated people go to a university for eight painful years to become an expert in it. Usually when you spend eight years in school, you can sew a heart back together or help a serial killer walk free. Eight years in economics sounds as fascinating as a 15-volume encyclopedia set about the history of yawning.

They say *a fool and his money are soon parted.* Consider me an exhibit A in the example. The dumbest thing I ever spent money on was a keyboard vacuum. I got it at a gift/trinket shop when I was like 13 years old. I had money to burn and saw the vacuum and bought it. I didn't own a computer with a keyboard, or a typewriter or anything to use the stupid thing on. It was just this tiny vacuum cleaner with a little motor that hummed and sucked up crumbs into a little black fabric bag on the side. Actually, now that I think about it, the vacuum was pretty cool. Wish I had it today. But it's sad that a 13-year-old couldn't find something better to use the money on… like comic books or drugs.

They say *money doesn't make you rich,* which is another ironic statement about wealth not enriching one's life. Again, this statement was definitely made by a trust fund asshole that was snorting cocaine off the tits of a $5,000-an-hour prostitute. You can bet your bottom dollar that any quote about money was made by someone with a lot of money. Any quote stating you don't need money or that it's not important was absolutely made by someone so rich, they could wipe their ass with Ben Franklin's face.

And if you hear anyone claim that money won't buy happiness, feel free to give them my home address, where I will greet them warmly before kicking them in the dick.

AND OTHER FUNNY STORIES

THE DEATH OF OUR DREAMS

BOMBA
THE BULLSHIT ARTIST

In the summer of 1981, my family rented a house on Shelter Island — a choice mound of land between the north and south forks of eastern Long Island. Shelter Island is accessible only by ferry... keeping away the riff raff of the world. The ratty, split-level blue box we chartered was a scamper away from the beach where my cousins and I would terrorize the neighborhood during the entire month of July. At the time, we probably rented the place for half a week's paycheck. As a prime AirBNB hot spot today, you'd have to sacrifice your first-born child for a few rotten midweek days -- regardless of the weather. But we secured the place for an entire month and transformed the joint into our temporary jungle gym.

Preparing for the trip, I was assigned a job that is given to most 9-year-olds... securing the illegal fireworks. My buddy Adam handed me a paper list with the name of every screamer, banger and bomb you could possibly imagine – with a descriptor telling what each firework did in the sky.

I checked off what I needed and after a few weeks, Adam returned with a crate full of colorful rockets. I exchanged the $40 my father had given me for my fair share of the pile. Our July was to start, quite literally, with a bang!

On Independence Day, after being in our rented home for only a few short days, we were blowing the place to smithereens with cherry bombs and firecrackers – an incursion that I'm sure made the permanent residents delirious with joy. Between all the aunts, uncles and cousins... as well as visitors, kids and their cousins, the overstuffed animal house had people bursting from the windows. The local fire marshal would have frowned in disapproval at both the illegal fireworks and the human capacity quota.

As the day fell into night on the fourth of July, my father started the highly anticipated firework show.

First up -- after the prerequisite Rob Roys over ice -- were the Helicopters: large, Tylenol capsule-like tubes with wings and fuses. My father lit the first one and the whirligig fluttered into the sky with a head full of colorful sparks. It then bee-lined to the corner of the roof, which immediately caught on fire. Everyone on the raised deck panicked and knocked about like bowling pins. My Uncle John attempted to douse the flames with a strawberry daiquiri. By the time the men had constructed a chair tower to attack the flames at close range, my father was arcing an accurate stream of water with a garden hose from ground level -- dousing the fire in good time.

Next up on the show card was another Helicopter. Since the first had gone so swimmingly; why not try another? So my father lit the unpredictable grenade, which zipped like a gunshot across the ground and exploded under his friend's

Corvette Stingray. This prompted another mob panic where the men grabbed their car keys and pounced at the vehicles parked across the lawn. The Stingray didn't explode, but there was no point in taking any chances. The cars were quickly transferred into the street.

Skipping the small stuff, my father went right for the gleaming goods. The piéce de résistance! The 96 Shot Color Pearl. Slated for the end, we transferred the big grand finale to the grand opening. This powder-keg beast looked as though someone had lashed 30 coin rolls together in a circle and wrapped a label around it. Basically, a log of stumpy Roman candles - it was set to deliver a glowing flare up into the night sky, one at a time, until all 96 'pearls' had been released in a dazzling display.

My father set the black-powder log onto the lawn and lit the fuse. It sparkled brightly, sizzling along until it disappeared inside the keg… and stopped.

Few things set your heart racing more than a stagnant firework… maybe a tube of Pillsbury crescent rolls or an un-triggered Jack in the Box, but those don't blow your face off when they pop. 96 Shot Color Pearls do!

My father and I approached the idle candle to see what was the matter. Perhaps if he'd been armed with the hose, I wouldn't have been so nervous. But he was without water and I was skittish as a mouse. I couldn't handle the pressure any longer and bailed as my mind raced with a thousand scenarios… pirate eye-patch worn to school… ears blown off… or simply: The Man Without A Face. The last thing I saw as I dove into a bush was my dad leaning over the 96 Shot Color Pearl as a deafening WHOOOM filled the air. By then, I'd tucked and rolled and was back on my feet, safe behind a few leafy twigs. I caught the dark sky filled with all 96 shot colors pearls... their red glare, bursting in air. My father was on his ass, looking up in amazement, his face and handlebar moustache not mangled in any way.

The bomb left a small crater in the ground, but the house deck audience roared in applause! A fire department eventually came to see what all the boom was about, but quickly left when we assured them, we were done with our show. My father cracked a few dozen green light sticks and handed them out to the kids, which prompted us to run around the yard, twirling them about without any fear of fire hazards or yard-cratering explosives.

Perhaps the nuclear green glow sticks would deform us in the years to come, but that was a problem to deal with another day.

•••

The summer of '81 was a glorious one. The sun seemed to shine every day. *Raiders of the Lost Ark* was riding high in the theaters, and *For Your Eyes Only* had just been released -- my favorite James Bond movie. We rode our bikes around the island like it was our own private obstacle course, and we tackled an ice cream shop named Foxy's every chance we could.

Our caddy-corner neighbors were a French family who took a bungalow right on the pink, shell-lined shore. John, with long sandy hair and glistening tan skin was the 11-year-old boy I occasionally ran with. My skin was paper white and usually turned red, but by mid-summer, my epidermis had sun-grilled and rested into a nice, golden hue.

Most notable about John and his single mother was the fact the she and her sister sunbathed topless all day. Something that caught the attention of... well, everyone! One afternoon an aggressive boat wave washed me into a tumble and coughed me up at the feet of the complacent French women... their fabulous ta-tas poking at me like four, sun-ripened bananas. My mother had to holler from our encampment a few yards away to break my gaze. You would have thought as an adult I'd be a breast man, but I much prefer the legs and butt, something that was also hanging noticeably from their tiny French bikinis.

After a week, we'd grown so accustomed to seeing their browning tits in all their exposed glory, that they became as commonplace as the rippling ocean... no more sexualized than an elbow or the massive gut of the old fisherman a few houses down who cast a line out with nothing to show for it but a drunken sunburn and an empty cooler that once contained rows of Pabst Blue Ribbon beer.

Exposure... to the sun or to naked breasts is how many countries apply the social ointment of taking the sting out of taboo subjects... legalization of marijuana, topless sunbathing, and perhaps even wine drinking for children at the dinner table. Americans tend to be prudes about certain subjects like that, yet we're also the world's biggest producers of porn, so it's a dichotomy that is constantly fighting itself.

Ironically, Neil Diamond's *America* was a smash hit that summer and the radio blared the chorus "We're coming to America... TODAY!" so precisely on the half hour, you could set the drink blender to it. Friends and family came to visit in a never-ending parade of Hawaiian shirts, extra-large lollipop treats and relaxing vacation sighs. Young faces stood determined in wafting clouds of smoke, waiting for the grill to dispense a crispy wiener onto a fresh bun to fuel the hyper-active adrenaline that would catapult us into the night... until ice pops could be administered as a sugar rush night cap.

Flipping through a People magazine, I set on an article about the summer's Worsts... Worst sex symbol was Woody Allen, and the song with the worst lyrics was The Police's *Dee Do Do Do, De Da Da Da*. The radio informed us that our beloved fellow Long Islander, Harry Chapin died in a fiery car crash on the Long Island Expressway. *Cat's In The Cradle* became the unofficial melancholy anthem as we watched sunsets hit the horizon in a different way.

My father and I played golf on a public course that was no greener than the lapping shore of our sun-crisp beach strip. After a while, a month in a strange house felt like an eternity. We took to hitting garage sales and chatting with the locals to break up the monotony of listening to the pack of tipsy adults we'd come to the island with... as well as each other.

After we'd turned the cranks of every gumball machine on the island, we began a clear sweep of every Saturday yard sale we could reach by bike. Our last few days on the island, we hit a long driveway that was littered with piles of moldy crap on cheap folding tables. Living on an island, it's hard to unload your unwanted junk on people, as it's a self-contained area. Your stuff doesn't travel far and the clientele don't travel from all the nooks of the world. So, your customers are just your friends and neighbors in the immediate vicinity.

We combed over the stuff at the bountiful sale when I discovered stacks of yellowing books with covers that were in various stages of wear. I picked one up and read the cover. *Bomba the Jungle Boy.*

"Great book" the house owner said, sliding up to me with a grin. He respectfully clasped his hands behind his back and leaned over the book table and pointed with his nose.

"All these books are wonderful. Bomba the Jungle Boy was my favorite book series as a kid!" I thumbed the pages of *Bomba the Jungle Boy* and nodded. The cover was vintage pulp art of a loin-clothed, Tarzan-like white boy and a leopard doing some kind of ritualistic dance on a gnarly patch of jungle.

Researching these books today, you find that they were written by a nameless committee under the pseudonym Roy Rockwood, which sounds like a character that could wander into the frame of a *Flintstone's* cartoon. According to our finest research resource Wikipedia: "A common theme of the Bomba books is that Bomba, because he is white, has a soul that is awake, while his friends, the dark-skinned natives, have souls that are sleeping."

With this kind of philosophy drilled into the minds of porous white kids across the U.S. in the 1920s, it shouldn't be any wonder why race relations have been a steaming pile of rubble for the past 100 years since its printing.

I don't remember how the book transaction went down. I'm pretty sure I dropped all my coins in gumball machines, leaving my pockets empty. My cheeks were filled with colorful balls of gum, so he probably gave me the book for free... or my friend Ray gave me a nickel to purchase it with. I proudly took Bomba back to the house and displayed the book to my family, showing them that despite the fact that I was a terrible student, I was bettering myself by reading ancient, racist books, before tossing it into my suitcase.

By then, John had been long gone -- back to France with his family. The two little boys who vacationed directly across the street were gone as well. Their pot-bellied fishing grandpa had entertained them for weeks, but it was time for them to move on as well. The only trace of them was a little cap gun and holster they left behind that their father claimed I stole... hanging naked and forgotten on a large bush. We collected everything we'd accumulated on the trip... bags filled with ribbed seashells scooped by the seashore... Cracker Jack prizes accrued from the bottom of every box... and pounds of sand that were in every crevice of every item we owned.

Shirts were dragged back onto our salty skin and sneakers were shoehorned onto our swollen feet. Like Bomba, we'd been free to roam without a care... playing in the waves, windsurfing in the easy breeze and dancing with the playful leopards of our imaginations. Although Bomba appeared to swing though the vines of some South American jungle playground, we tore through the neighborhoods of middle-class suburbanites on BMX bikes.

It was time to return to civilized life and there was nothing we could do about it. We piled into our station wagon and left Shelter Island quieter than we came... crispy, like a basket of fried clam strips served in chipper, red-netted plastic baskets.

•••

The following school year was 5th grade and I had one of my most memorable teachers. A grandmotherly woman named Mrs. Bucolo. Set to retire at the end of the year, she was a wonderful, inspirational teacher full of love and caring. When I brought an oil painting from the private art class I took, she beamed with pride, declared me the next Norman Rockwell and doted on me like a grandchild. My confidence went through the roof and I became a different person. She encouraged me in every way and my grades shot up the boards.

After she retired, she did what most 77-year-olds do… went to Florida. The allure of high temperatures and low taxes is too hard to resist. Backbreaking snow isn't kind to anyone over 40, so you might as well get out of New York while the gettin' is good. Mrs. Bucolo and I corresponded by mail -- exchanging lively letters for a few months until they suddenly stopped. I feared she had died, but realized quickly that she wanted to enjoy her golden years in peace and quiet without some snot-nosed brat with the panache to paint, tossing mail at her every week.

The summer of 1982, from what I remember, was uneventful. There was no island getaway or frolicking barefoot with the French by the shore. I remember *E.T. The Extra-Terrestrial* was in the theaters and talking about it with some friends at a pool party. We definitely spent many sweltering days glued to the TV in our cool basement, bending our forearms into bows, yanking the joysticks of our Atari 2600. But other than that… a total memory wash.

The following school year was 6th grade. The last year I'd be at the elementary school before going to junior high. I went from Mrs. Bucolo, the warm and tender grandma who was a cornerstone to my young schooling foundation, to Mr. Kregler, a stone wall.

An ex-navy man, Mr. Kregler radiated the charm one might expect of a gruff old sailor in a room full of rambunctious children. His comfort in the classroom mirrored Mrs. Bucolo's comfort manning a 25-caliber deck gun bolted to the bow of an armored patrol boat. Every day he wore his black navy cap down over his shaded eyes... its brim coated in military scrambled eggs, showing each of us who was boss. His face was a grey cube of granite where his bulbous nose protruded out like a pasty chicken drumstick.

Fresh into the new year I tested Mr. Kregler with my wise-ass comic stylings, which he did not appreciate one iota. My desk was immediately pushed up against the chalkboard, where I faced a wall of smudgy green for the rest of the year... my back to the class. He would have stuck me in front of the chalkboard in the far-left corner behind the filing cabinet, but someone was already there.

Chip Fusaro. Chip had already tested Mr. Kregler's limits and found himself crammed into the dusty corner.

Shockingly, I had not been paying attention when Chip tested Mr. Kregler's limits with his own comic stylings and got himself jammed into oblivion. Chip and I became fast friends and we used the chalkboard's chalk tray to slide notes to each other throughout the year.

Rounding out Kregler's Kriminal tri-fecta, on my

right, was Adam Anderson, the guy who made sure our Shelter Island trip was stacked with exploding fireworks. Mr. Kregler made quick examples of us: that tomfoolery would not be accepted in his class! That lesson was accepted by the others, but Chip, Adam and I lived an entirely different school experience. Since Mr. Kregler had his back to us, he never once saw a note slide or a face made in mocking gesture. I'm not sure the three of us were ever part of the class or absorbed one lesson. We enjoyed the kind of freedom that you rarely experience in school... outside the watchful eye of authority.

We knew early on what kind of man Mr. Kregler was. The first major assignment was a bird watching project. Walking about in nature, we were to find and document 10 birds in the wild, then research and write about them. As a 50 year-old man, this is a Zen project that today I'd attack with zeal. But as a coltish 11 year-old scallywag, this yawn-inducing assignment went over like a lead balloon. Since I rarely looked up in the sky, I took to drawing birds I found in our encyclopedia set that was so old, half the birds were extinct by the time I gained ownership of it.

Having my bird diary returned, I was pleased with my B+ grade, yet confused as to how my beautifully detailed bird renderings didn't grade higher. Apparently, my drawing of a colorful and tropical Kingfisher was met with praise, but was proven unlikely to be found bouncing on the boughs of my barren New York backyard in the blustery autumn breezes.

Also failing to reach the status of an A grade was my report on Borneo. Even though it had a beautifully illustrated map, with detailed mountain ridges, roads and a legend indicating its plentiful resources such as gas and poverty, it failed to push its grade above a B+. Again, turning to my ancient encyclopedia set, I presented as many facts about Borneo as I could muster without having to go to the library, a place I found not only intimidating, but downright confusing.

I'm sure the local library would have given me some choice content to use for the report instead of the sparse paragraph from the encyclopedia when Borneo most likely didn't even have electricity upon its printing.

•••

When winter came, so did the next school assignment... a book report. I'm sure during the cold winter, Mr. Kregler was hunkered down tightly with Mrs. Kregler, nipping on warm coco and yanking books off a four-foot pile next to his lazy-boy recliner. I, on the other hand, was not planning on doing any kind of reading. I was determined to be outside in the snow... building forts, stacking towering snowmen and sledding over jumps that would toss me far enough to break a bone.

Books don't handle well in the wet snow and they're not convenient to hold while tobogganing at intense angles.

I'd never done a book report before. At least, not that I remembered. I wasn't sure how to tackle it. Most teachers seem to think a book report is born into our subconscious muscle memory... like swallowing. They command, "Do a book report!" and scoot us away to our personal, first-edition libraries. I wasn't a strong reader and Mr. Kregler probably finished a book or two before breakfast.

As you can imagine, I let the assignment fall by the

wayside. I tend to work well under pressure. Some people do. If given an absurd deadline, I'll rise to the challenge and make it work. It's part of my DNA. But trying to digest an entire book and write a book report on said book two days before it's due is tough to accomplish, even for a thin children's book. Most of my fellow students had not only secured a book to read, but were mostly done with their reports by the time I realized I needed to do one. They'd gone to the library and chosen books. I wasn't quite sure where our school library was located or if we even had one. And if we did have one, how many books could they have? Four or five? By that point the selection would be limited.

So, I did what I always did best... skipped the reading altogether and completely bullshitted my way through a totally made-up book plot. This is the procedure of the undisciplined student with horrible study habits. And what book did I choose as the basis of this fabricated story? Why, everyone's favorite superior-raced, jungle-dwelling cracker... Bomba the Jungle Boy!

Panicking in my bedroom, I turned to my mostly barren bookshelf -- its offerings were slim. Mostly science picture books, art books and joke books. But there was *Bomba the Jungle Boy*... calling out like Tarzan to rescue me.

I couldn't tell you what the hell *Bomba the Jungle Boy* was about because I didn't read it then, nor have I read it to this day. But I'm sure it was no more nuanced than a B-Grade comic book. But let me tell you, A.J. Schmitz's version of Bomba the Jungle Boy was quite the doozy. The plot analysis went something like this...

Bomba, as most white children are named, was just a regular kid who wanted to do his own thing... but his father wouldn't let him! Geez, a story snatched right from the headlines of real life! He probably wanted to play on the beach and surf all day, but his stupid father wanted him to get an education in school! So Bomba did what most kids do when their parents are cramping their style. They run away from home into the jungle. I'm sure Bomba tossed a hobo sack over his shoulder and made his way to the nearest jungle... as most kids are wont to do. Considering most jungles require two airliners and a puddle jumper to get to them, Bomba seemed to find one conveniently in his hometown.

Bomba's father, finding a note about Bomba abandoning the family for the freedom of the jungle, goes mad with rage and grabs the nearest shotgun. His father trails Bomba in hot pursuit in what becomes a series of vignettes that play like Richard Connells book *The Most Dangerous Game*. Dad keeps shooting and Bomba keeps getting away by the skin of his teeth -- tree branches blasting to pieces as the tension rises. Eventually, dad catches up to Bomba and guns him down in cold blood. A scene where the dad clutches his steely gun and gently weeps at his regretful actions is particularly moving.

I can't actually remember how the book report closed out. I imagine there was some reflection about uncontained rage, complicated father/son relationships, and perhaps the freedom of living in the jungle. One thing that did NOT appear in the book, was anything about a leopard, which seems odd as Bomba is right on the cover, dancing with a leopard. Not only that, Bomba the Jungle Boy is a series of books that continues for 20 mind-numbing adventures. The fact that I kill him off in book one of the series shines a spotlight on my credibility as a reader.

Also of note was the fact that the book report needed to be three pages, ratcheting up the bullshit factor even higher. I'm sure a normal book report handed in by me, of a book that I actually read, would be clearly written and concise. But when you're totally winging it, you tend to bend the bullshit to the extreme. You overwrite, construct complicated run-on sentences and use incredibly complicated words in hopes of filling up space.

Having just made parameters with a third page that was 90% blank, I tucked my hand-written, loose sleeve pages into covers of red construction paper and smiled. I confidently wrote Bomba the Jungle Boy in thick black letters across the front and handed in my book report on time with the rest of the responsible, well-read children.

•••

After an extended winter break, we returned to complete the next half of the school year. While staring at the green, freshly cleaned chalkboard, my vision was suddenly filled with red... the words BOMBA THE JUNGLE BOY written in my own hand, filling my eyes like a ghost. I looked up to see Mr. Kregler looming above me, returning my book report. His eyes twinkled under the brim of his Navy cap and there was a hint of a sneer at the corner of his mouth that rolled up under his bulbous proboscis. His arms were filled with the entire class's reports, so he spun away and continued the distribution process.

I gently brought the book report down to my lap and let the moment sink in. When I handed in the report, I felt a great sense of relief that I'd gotten the assignment in on time. I'd walked away with a clear mind and a light heart... ready to enjoy the break. But now that the report was back in my hands, I realized with terror what I did was absolutely fraudulent. The heavy weight that I felt the night before the report was due came crashing back down on my lungs like sand bags.

As the class murmured behind me -- everyone in a tizzy over their grades, I searched my feelings and looked inward. How bad could the grade be? An F minus? An F minus minus?? Jail?! The worst punishment of course, which had occurred many times in my life, was the need for my parents to SIGN the failed assignment so that everyone could document with legal signatures, the paper trail of an education going completely wrong. One time in 3rd grade I told my father that we were having a signature contest in class and that he should enter. I took that signature, which he gave freely without question, and pinned it to the failed math test, which was accepted by my teacher for some unknown reason.

But this... this was a book report!

There was no way to hide this red-covered monstrosity! This was a book of failure. Not a pop quiz that shakes the foundations of the unprepared. Not a test after one night of studying. This was a slow-moving car wreck! I had MONTHS to prepare for this. So much time to do it right, I could have read a book series and done a paper long enough to be entered into a professional journal. But I blew it off and committed writer's suicide by making up a story. And not even a believable story at that! The father kills Bomba? What is going on here? I obviously watched The Road Warrior too many times! If a snow day had delayed the report an extra day, I probably would have added a nuclear holocaust to the storyline and had Bomba and his father fighting together over a fresh dog leg with a Cyclops who was determined to eat dinner as well.

Finally, I cracked my book report and flipped to the back. In the middle of that nearly blank third page... dead center... in Kregler's distinctive scripty handwriting was a large red C, with the notation: "Bomba the Jungle Boy was my favorite book series as a kid."

I closed the cover and nodded. Before I could let the grade sink in, someone was on top of me asking me what my grade was. I sheepishly told them. But it didn't matter. I realized later that a C was absolutely... AWESOME! Mr. Kregler knew straight up that everything I wrote was bullshit, yet he gave me a C.

In reality, the grade was an A.

As a report based on a book I read, it was a clear F. But as a creative writing assignment? An easy A! So he kindly split the difference and gave me a C. Total win on my end.

My view of Mr. Kregler changed completely after that. The bullshit Bomba book report was the beginning for sure. But then he moved everyone's desks to the outer edges of the room and created a large Skelly game board on the floor using colored tape. Skelly is a game played on the ground, in a big box... like a monopoly board, using pieces you slide like checkers or weighted bottle caps. We'd have epic Skelly competitions during the cold winter days, which made for a fun classroom environment. Mr. Kregler was a city kid who'd run the streets of Manhattan like you see in ancient black and white photos, where kids were filthy and worked in black-lung factories.

When he asked if anyone had John Dennis Fitzgerald's *Great Brain* books, I raised my hand. I brought the series in and Mr. Kregler read them to us in the afternoons in his warm timber, which captivated us completely.

Upon later reflection, I realized that the soft nature of Mrs. Bucolo and the hard edge of Mr. Kregler weren't so different after all. In fact, they were almost the same. Two tough, warm-hearted grandparent figures. Cornerstones in my youthful education.

.

CROSSTOWN TRAFFIC

Sandwiched between San Diego and Sonoma Valley is a sleepy little town called Los Angeles. People claim that L.A. is a fantastic place to live, which is true... if it was 1940... well before the city's population exploded to 150 billion people. It's a desert town that butts directly up against the ocean. A magical place. Unfortunately, every man, woman, and child, regardless of economic standing, owns nine cars and inexplicably drives them all at the same time, at every moment of the day.

One fine L.A. day, I was sunning on an empty beach in Malibu with some friends. As the sun began to fall, we prepared ourselves to hit a restaurant up the road. A famous joint named after a guy who wore a panama hat and sunglasses... or something like that.

We'd called ahead with reservations and a menu wish list. We had visions of arriving at the place to a smiling staff displaying glistening rainbow cocktails in sweating glasses with umbrellas and large triangles of hacked fruit jammed into the rim like a bevy of diving beauties, waiting to jack-knife into a vodka concoction like a vaudeville movie. But of most importance, at least to me, was the mission's primary goal. Something I'd been looking forward to all day. One of those ridiculous, multi-tiered seafood towers with crustaceans from every seaside port, chilled on tiny beds of slivered ice, perfectly plumped and waiting to be devoured with an assortment of dipping sauce… all within my arm's reach.

Unfortunately, it was not to be. Some wealthy Troglodyte managed to smash his expensive car into another expensive car on the Pacific Coast highway, cutting off our safe passage to the restaurant with a gnarly traffic jam whose effects are probably still being felt today. Leaving the beach parking lot, I watched a man in a convertible sports car yank down his cap and nestle into his leather bucket seat for a long winter's nap. Obviously, this was not the first row of traffic he'd been in and certainly not his last. My dream of watching the sunset while perched on a balcony dangling over the Pacific Ocean with a pile of chilled shrimp, evaporated into thin air.

In place of that dream was a reconstituted nightmare of a Venice Beach scene, where a homeless man, whose DNA consisted of mostly sand, yanked some kind of crust out of his ass through his filthy trousers while barking at skateboarders sitting atop a bench he once occupied. I choked down an avocado and tomato sandwich on flourless bread that was essentially nuts holding hands. I never forgave L.A. after that horrible incident, and I never will.

It's where my hatred of traffic grew from mild annoyance to a burning fire of rage that rots in the core of my soul.

I consider traffic to be one of the most truly horrible plagues to befall mankind. Unfortunately, it's all of our own making. The frustrating, endless grind of sitting in a car and inching towards a destination that feels unachievable in your lifetime, is a pain that can't be replicated in any simulation. Perhaps we can create a new word for the feeling of hopelessness it invokes. Trafalia? Gridoden? Clustfuckia?

It doesn't matter what time of the day or night you drive in Los Angeles... Sunday at 8:00 am, Friday at 5:00 pm. It's a constant, never-ending jumble of cars. Los Angeles and cars are so synonymous that people's cars are nicer than their houses. People put so much money, time and love into their cars they achieve art status... drivable masterworks of design and style. They zoom up to their houses and apartment buildings that are being held together with garbage bags and duct tape. If you're going to spend half your life in your car -- driving or sitting in traffic, you might as well be comfortable -- and do it in style.

I'm from Long Island, which has a highway called the Long Island Expressway. Deemed, 'the world's longest parking lot,' this nightmare of asphalt has been the bane of my existence since the day I was born. Its acronym is LIE, which is apropos because to call it an express to somewhere is the world's largest fib. Unless it's an express to your grave, which it will surely drive you to with stress and frustration. Los Angeles and New York City are bookend rivals to see who can drive its citizens to madness with road rage.

For some unknown reason, a gaggle of New York politicians in the 1920s gave a "visionary" named Robert Moses carte blanche to build a ton of bridges and roads all over the New York metropolitan area. Unfortunately, Moses didn't have the vision to see beyond the Ford Model T. Every road, tunnel and bridge seems to have been built for a car no larger than three feet wide with tires no thicker than a Tour de France bicycle. I believe Moses himself drove a car he wound with a key like a grandfather clock, and had wheel spokes made of wood. I don't know how else to explain the nature of our modern Long Island road system.

Every entrance ramp that leads you into roaring highway traffic is about 3 yards long and every exit ramp is a hellacious hairpin turn that is difficult to navigate for even a toddler on a tricycle. Getting off a swinging, bending road like The Northern State Parkway requires you to hit a sweeping blind hill that bends 20 degrees to the right at 65 miles an hour, then slam your breaks down to 25 and merge between cars that are getting *on* the Northern State Parkway in an area that is no larger than a standard putting green. How most of the roads on Long Island aren't a smoking pile of twisted metal and body parts is a mystery to me.

Unfortunately, not only did Robert Moses design and build these roads, he did it for decades. Besides being a horrible racist that killed thriving neighborhoods by laying highways through them, he alienated and segregated people with steel and concrete barriers. He laid twisted knots of roads and overpasses destined to be irrelevant before the concrete dried. This man said things like "Why don't we take a four-lane highway and merge it down to one?" and people thought that was an excellent idea and rubber-stamped it with approval. The cretins who thought that was an excellent idea were elected officials and it shows you the power of voting and getting the right people in charge of your general vicinity. It also shows you the power of money and what can happen when these cretins toss cash around like cheap confetti.

Moses, as well as a million other engineers didn't realize in the future we'd be screaming around the country in cars the size of small tanks, with the power to yank tree stumps from the garden with the tap of the foot. I live in a hilly town where the roads were formed by horse and carriage paths. It's a town made for a lazy Sunday drive around the water, yet most of the inhabitants drive cars that can go from zero to 60 in about 2.5 seconds. They're tooling around in $80,000 racing machines designed to blow the hair off your head with wind friction. Sadly, that can't be done in most places unless you live in the open country of Oklahoma. So to release that pent up speed racer anxiety, they open up their engine on the Long Island Expressway and blast down the highway doing 90. Where they're going so fast, no one knows. Maybe moving to a place that isn't choking on traffic day and night.

Of course, other parts of the USA have knots of hair-yanking traffic as well. One time on a visit to my uncle's house in Washington DC, we got jammed on the horrible road known as interstate 495. This road was smartly designed to go around the DC metro area in a large, circle pattern. That is smart thinking, except for some unknown reason it's just a large circular pile of traffic all the time. They made the road really big, which somehow just made the traffic bigger. During this particular jam sometime in the mid 80s, we'd been stopped for so long, people got out of their cars and began bar-b-quing. It blossomed into a blacktop block party. Beers were cracked and Frisbees were tossed with complete freedom. We became emotionally attached to the people in other cars and when the asphalt artery unclogged and began to move, the radios squelched and people waved tearful goodbyes like soldiers going off to war.

Gnarly, spirit-crushing traffic is not exclusive to the United States. Not by a long stretch. Visiting my wife's family in Brazil, they had a great idea to take a drive and show me around the city of Sao Paulo. It was very thoughtful of them. Sao Paulo, if you've never been, is a city that literally doesn't end. I think the reason the city didn't expand further than its current size is the Atlantic ocean was on one side and Paraguay was on the other. In the dictionary next to the term "Urban Sprawl" there's a picture of Sao Paulo, Brazil.

I remember the first time I flew into Sao Paulo. I had a choice window seat and watched as we descended into the city. I was convinced that someone had mounted a giant printed city scroll over the window and was just rolling it by hand across my view. Building after building, street after city street, continued on and on across my eyes. Considering planes, even when slowing down to land, still go about 200 miles an hour, the amount of city unfolding before my eyes through that window was dumbfounding. After a solid ten minutes, I'm not sure I saw a fraction of it.

During this lovely drive as the afternoon folded into night, a football match between the Sao Paulo Football Club and the Palmerias Football Club ended and people flooded the streets like a military coup. Cars, people and dogs meandered through the highways like the apocalypse had come.

It was every man, woman and child for themselves. We sat in a cramped car for what seemed like a week and slowly, and most definitely not surely, crept back to my sister-in-law's house. It took about 4 hours. What ramped up the fun factor of this scenic adventure were the fans launching fireworks at one another through the windows of their cars. Roman candles and small bombs exploding around us as casually as one might honk the horn. I can only imagine what would have happened if their team lost. It was similar to a war zone except instead of people screaming in terror as exploding blasts of colorful light rained down on them, they laughed with glee as their eardrums ruptured in their skulls.

Sao Paulo is a city with endless cars and endless traffic, but it is the opposite in many ways to Los Angeles, another city that doesn't seem to end. The people of Sao Paulo don't live for their cars. Cars in Sao Paulo are like tools. They're pieced together like most people scrap together dinner from refrigerator leftovers. In many ways it's like America in 1977. The Brazilians are all driving 35-year-old cars, without any emissions laws and the roadside is littered with people working on their cars. The hoods are up and their asses are sticking out of the engine block as they crank some kind of gearshift or tighten a belt. They're shouting at the guy behind the wheel "is this doing anything?" while they twist or pinch an engine part to further the cause of getting them back on the road and to their destination.

These cars have been synthesized from pieces of other cars and parts of things that are not cars at all. Whatever tube, hose, rod or gear fits the engine and gets the cars puttering back on the road is good enough. It's possible most Brazilians are driving around with half an air conditioner under the hood.

Shockingly, the United States doesn't even crack many lists of the world's worst traffic. Many of those honors go to Europe, where people drive cars the size of go-carts, on roads formed when Alexander the Great was 'just pretty good,' and then reconstructed a million times over after half the cities were bombed to smithereens in two world wars.

The worst traffic happens in India, where multiple, six-lane highways crash together in a series of intersections without traffic lights, where cars pour head-first into a vehicle battlefield like the movie *Braveheart*. Designed with the ox and cart in mind, these roads attempt to squeeze millions of cars through an area that can handle about 100. Watching a video of these places is enough to inflict associative anxiety. Ramping up the stress factor is the zooming motorbikes, mopeds, auto-bikes and tuk-tuks that seem to fly through without any regard for life or limb. Toss in giant buses that make obnoxious wide turns and moves at a turtle's pace and it's a recipe for a mental breakdown.

Making traffic around the world unbearable regardless of hemisphere is the migraine inducing construction. The planet is in a constant state of repair. Planning on taking a nice road trip? Then you're guaranteed to be funneled into a one-lane highway as yellow-vested workers glue a crumbling bridge back together. Your careful plans of a five-hour trip turns to seven, and your ass has lost all its sensation.

During the pandemic of 2020, the entire world locked themselves into their homes and braced themselves for what may come. No one was on the road for years. I once drove to my sister's... a normal 2-hour drive, in about and hour and 15 minutes flat. Did we take advantage of these empty roads and get masses of workers out there fixing our decaying infrastructure? Of course not! They waited until sanctions were lifted and the streets were flooded again with honking, scrambling, impatient drivers. By then, the roads were at their worst so they needed to double the work crews, assuring citizens they'd be stuffed into a series of cement troughs like steel cattle going to the kill.

I hope to some day be fabulously wealthy so I can be carted around in a giant limo and excuse myself from the daily battle of traffic jams.

Avoiding people who are not only bad drivers, but most likely certifiably insane is a luxury I'm willing to pay a premium price for. My driver would be free to yell at anyone who cuts him off -- putting *his* face in the line of potential gunfire that he risks enduring by rolling down his window and barking at others. I'll hopefully be safe in the back -- drinking cool beverages and watching the world go by while watching TV, listening to music and hopefully not thinking about any kind of traffic, other than the band Traffic, which has some pretty good songs.

PASSWORDZ_33!$

I bought a new phone for my son and I put him on my billing plan. I figured that would make everything nice and convenient because we'd be on the same plan and it would eliminate complications in our already confusing and bitterly uncontrollable lives.

I'm kidding... our lives are not confusing.

But what I thought was going to be simplicity, turned into more complications. We had to make an on-line AT&T account and that meant one thing... More PASSWORDS!

I can't even keep track of all the passwords I have *now*, let alone another one. I guess this is the price we pay for modern technology. I do just about everything online and the convenience is bar none. I don't have to deal with bank lines or snooty people in the wild. I don't have to hold for the next available agent or write endless checks by hand. It's pretty amazing.

I have an App on my iPhone that keeps track of all my

passwords. I have passwords for PayPal, credit cards, insurance, health providers, Amazon, Facebook, Twitter, email... and about 159 others. Hopefully I won't forget the password to the iPhone App that holds all these passwords or I'd be seriously screwed.

Actually, I don't know the password for that app at all. I actually have all my passwords on a piece of paper in my desk. I've been working on computers for over 30 years and I have passwords written on paper like some kind of goddamn knuckle-dragging NeanderTHALL. Perhaps I'd be better served chiseling the passwords into stone! I could eventually present them to a museum council who will accept them and place them among other ancient artifacts... like my fax machine.

But the number of log-in names and passwords I have is just ridiculous. Sometimes I have to log into a site that I only plan to use once and never use again. That's annoying because I start getting emails from them when I could care less about their damn wares. I get emails from a printing company I used three years ago and although I've asked to be removed from their mailing list, I still get them. I did a "guess the Oscar winners" contest last year and now I'm part of this film forum email subscription thingy. I've been asked to be removed—no such luck. I even get a random email or two from Ben & Jerry's because I wanted some free ice cream at one point. Now I'm plagued by their emails even though I've removed myself from their email list about four times. Nothing in life is free!!

Sometimes these email lists ask you why you're leaving their list. Why do I have to tell you why I'm leaving your list? I didn't sign up for the fucking list! Sorry your feelings are hurt.

"Why are you leaving our list?" It's just not working anymore, ok? It's not you it's me. I'm seeing other email lists. Hope you can find a new email to fill the void.

While online shopping, I've checked out as a guest because I'm certain I'll never use the site again and a few months later, I'm checking out as a guest again -- wondering why I didn't create an account the first time. It's because of passwords, that's why. I know my computer logs some of them in automatically, but if I need to use a different computer, I need that password documented some other way.

I've gone through the whole process of signing up to a site only for the site to tell me that the email is already in the system. So, I'm already a customer! Then you need to find THAT password. This happens with job posting sites. You upload your resume, then they ask you to enter the same information that's on your resume. It's infuriating! By the time you finish, you'd rather be unemployed and living under a heroin bridge downtown than do it again.

Sometimes in our desire to make our lives easier, we end up making them harder, or at least, just as complicated. I may get less paper in the mail from my bank, which saves trees, but yesterday I got two letters from Chase promoting a credit card. TWO! Why two? There go those trees I just saved by doing my on-line banking. And even though I do all my banking on-line, my bank still sends me a bank statement once in a while that says "Paperless Billing" on the envelope. Really? Paperless, huh? I think I heard another tree fall in the forest.

Companies always suggest using different names and passwords and sometimes it's hard to think of creative names when you're working on the fly. A lot of times it's your name, or your nickname of some sort with some relevant numbers -- like your birthday backwards or you wife's birthday. Sometimes you completely forget a password and you have to ask them to email it to you. Then you get it and you're like "Oh, yea, now I remember. Boy, that's a pretty stupid password."

Sometimes you have to answer the personal question that you've created for yourself to prove it's you. My favorite question is "What's your favorite restaurant?" Well, considering I made this account 7 years ago and now I live in a different city and have enjoyed 321 restaurants since then, I have no idea! Then you fail that question and get another one like "what's your sister's birth city?" or "What's your favorite sports team?" Sometimes these questions are difficult to answer and you're the idiot who came up with the answers!

Now certain sites have a "strength of password" indicator on the side where you enter a new password. You enter your new password name (that must contain at least one capital letter, a number and a special character) and a colored bar comes up telling you if your entire identity is within a hair's breadth of being stolen. A green bar means strong and red bar means weak. If the password is weak, you can add a bunch of stupid numbers and symbols at the end of the password... not only to confuse any hackers, but to guarantee you'll need to have your new password sent to you by email when you forget it.

They say special characters, but I'm not sure why

they're special. The exclamation mark is the same button as the number 1. How special is that? Is that going to stop a hacker getting into your nude photos and spreading them around the internet? I don't think so.

And what if you do have your new password sent to you by email. Is your email password strong enough to stop hackers from getting access to your email who can then, in turn, take that new password? It's like looking in a mirror, inside a mirror, inside a mirror....

The worst is when you have your password emailed to you, but the email is actually a URL link that diverts you to a site where you log in and change your password. That takes forever and half the time you end up remembering your password. Or you'll try and create a new password, and it tells you not to use the same password as last time! But I just tried it and it didn't work!

Many times you have to create a password and then immediately reenter the exact same thing directly below it. I think this is a test to see if you're either paying attention or a complete moron.

If you forget your password, some companies make you create a new password and bring you to a page where the first box says 'Enter your old password'. I wouldn't be here if I remembered my old password, you horrible, soulless interface!

If you work in an office, sometimes the company makes you change the password to your computer every quarter. That's a pain in the ass! Unless you're working in the Pentagon, it's completely unnecessary. I doubt your computer is holding vital information that will topple your company, so why change the password? Why even HAVE a password? When you're out sick and someone needs something on your computer, don't they call you at home anyway to get your password? Most people just write their password on a post-it note and stick it to the monitor! Talk about high security.

People become so fed up entering passwords that they simply write PASSWORD as their password. If they really get adventurous, they might write password 1 as their password. Or Password with a capital P. But even this is hard to figure out if you're just the common man. Sit in front of your friend's computer and stare at that blinking password log-in space. Have any idea as to what they could possibly have as their password? Of course not! Even the best detectives can't figure it out. You could probably do weeks of CSI-type character study break-downs and still not figure it out. And if you did figure out the name, like your friend the dog lover's password is "doggybreath," how would you know it's not doggybreath7621, or doggybreath90210 or some other number variable? You could be there for months trying to log on.

We spend so much time making complicated passwords that by now we can probably just use 1234 as a password and it would be fine. How many hackers actually think to enter something so basic? I guess these computer bad guys have software that generates algorithms that breaks-down thousands of number and word combinations in seconds so 1234 may get them in your computer in about 5 seconds. And if they do, what are they getting? My credit card info? Someone charged an HD flat screen to my Visa once and I called the credit card company to claim it wasn't my charge. They removed the charges within seconds, but seemed completely disinterested in trying to track down the people who did it even though they had the address where the TV was shipped to! Well, if they don't care if fraudulent charges are flying around, why should I? As long as I get my money back, I guess.

I logged into Facebook back in 2008 and I haven't needed to log back in yet. I couldn't even begin to tell you what my password is for that. What was I doing in 2008 that could place me in the password ballpark? Skeet shooting? Naked Duck, Duck, Goose? The possibilities are endless. Some sites log you out if you blink. That's good and bad. Good if it's a banking site because it's possible someone could slide into your seat .005 seconds after you get up, and start transferring your money into their off-shore account.

They've upped the security game even further with password changing. Now they text you a code that you need to enter. I get panicked that I won't do it fast enough and it will reset. Once in a while a password changing interface will ask if I want them to send me a code by text or phone call. Phone call? What year is this… 1982? I've been trying to avoid phone calls for the past 10 years. Send me a text!

Google likes to tell me that someone entered my password on a new computer, which is usually the computer that I've being using for the past six years. They'll email me at my main email and my backup email so as to lather me into a frenzy of paranoia. Then I get worried if I was the one that actually logged in or if it was someone else at the EXACT time as me -- possibly siphoning my precious info from my computer with a link.

Google's email says that someone logged in from a certain location, and it's a location from the town next to me, but not EXACTLY my town. Which makes me worried. What are the chances someone a few towns over hacked my computer at 5:36 PM when I was logging onto my computer at 5:36 as well? It's possible I guess.

My phone scans my face and I'm instantly in and ready to tap an app or look at porn. If my face is not available for some reason, it asks for my code, which I've made the same number because I'm usually in a rush to respond to a worthless text, or find out who won Super Bowl XI because I'm in a bar full of guys who are dying to know the answer.

Technology has advanced beyond the point of wireless where you don't even need to type or speak. They have word programs that can track your eye movements and type things for you. They have voice boxes that can speak for you by reading your mind. These AI programs will search your cranium but still won't be able to find the password to your Taco Bell ordering app. If we're not careful, they could convert us to cyborgs.

Computers track us and know what we like. It's gone way beyond entering emails and passwords. I think my phone knows what I'm thinking. I looked for a Jets hat the other day on a hat website, and when I opened my Facebook feed, it displayed the exact Jets hat that I was looking at. That's all fine, it's called retargeting advertising… but I was looking at a hat on my *friend's* computer, which was another town over. How'd THAT happen? But even worse, my wife and I were talking about joining a gym and sure as the sun rises, my phone started displaying an absurd amount of gym membership offers in my immediate area. Hmmmm... that's weird.

But the ultimate display of frightening technology, was when I was thinking about sushi and Japanese restaurants filtered into my social feed. SUSHI RESTAURANTS! That I was THINKING about! Not talking about. Not looking at online... thinking about in *my brain*. A sushi roll popped in my brain... my brain being a twisted ball of fleshy matter that runs on electricity, and it somehow talked to the social fabric of the universe, which turned that thought into an ad that popped up on my news feed. Think about that for a second... or maybe don't! Turn off your brains!

All I know is if a large, muscular man in sunglasses comes to my door holding a delivery of sushi and asks for Sarah Connor, I'll say "That's me" and let the cosmic universe take care of the rest.

THE AXE MURDER INN

Online reviews can be tricky to navigate. People selling items give incentives in exchange for positive reviews. "We'll send you a free flower pot if you review our flower pot!" A 50¢ gift can go a long way to manipulate the hearts of a customer.

My friend Mike Mehann has owned and operated many successful and excellent restaurants all over Long Island. One thing he and I have talked about over the years is people's proclivity to give bad reviews. When someone enjoys, or is even overjoyed by a great meal or dining experience, their reaction is to ride that high into the night. But if someone has waited too long for a table or found their burger to be cooked a shade less than their desired redness, their immediate reaction is to funnel their rage into a scathing online review and tell the world of their cruel mistreatment.

Review postings are sounding boards of anger. Rarely is a restaurant's 5-star reviews filled with positive re-enforcement about the waiter or the service. But should a waitress so much as treat the customer as anything less than their long-lost puppy, the customer will fly off the handle and dispense an acidic, indignant fable that rivals the darkest suicidal writers of world literature. Diners tend to yank stars from the rating on the most mundane issues... lack of napkins, the waiter forgetting a Sprite, and waiting too long to get the check.

"I would have given this place five stars but the hostess had a run in her stockings!"

Chefs with Michelin star ratings have received zero-star ratings from Karen in Indiana because she thought her duck breast would taste more like chicken. I once gave a place 5 stars because I ate the best steak sandwich I ever had, regardless of the fact the cheap margarita accompanying it tasted like dish-water lemonade. I want the place to stay in business so I can eat more steak sandwiches. I don't hack people off at the knees because my fork had a hard water stain on it.

As a result, I take online reviews with a grain of salt. A 5-star review of a universally loved restaurant is probably 4-1/2 and a cheap diner that is 3-1/2 stars is probably closer to a 4. So when I booked a few nights in one of Stowe, Vermont's cheapest "hotels," I over-looked the 3-star rating as a terribly misunderstood 4. Maybe a 3-1/2 at best. Having improperly planned our ski trip, I was desperate to fill two nights near the mountain so we didn't have to sleep in the car. I had two choices... a $1,400 a night chalet, or a $200 a night "hotel." You can guess which one I chose.

This choice was met with instant disappointment under the roof that I currently sleep in. Grabbing the phone, my wife rattled off the bad reviews with a betrayal usually reserved for men who have romantic affairs.

"Do not rent a room here under any circumstances!" "Find a cardboard box to sleep in!" "This place is disgusting." These were reviews I could work with and turn in my favor.

"People tend to overreact to these things. They're all a bunch of spoiled rich folks expecting the best!" I pleaded. "It's a place to rest out heads for a few nights. No big deal!"

My wife was not convinced. "Dirty is dirty! I don't want bed bugs again!" she cries. And she's absolutely right. I can't handle another battle with the blood-sucking bed bugs either. I'm using bug-fighting money on this trip to Stowe. If we get bed bugs, I'll be forced to burn our entire village down, house by house and claim ravaging wild fires to the insurance company.

One online review claims the place is like *The Shining*, which is preposterous as the place in The Shining was a massive, sprawling estate. The photos of this place easily resemble the backwoods slaughterfest of *Friday the 13th*. So right off the bat, our reviewers can't be trusted with proper film comparisons. These elitist reviewers are accustomed to eunuchs feeding them grapes on sun-soaked beaches. Can't they go one day without 1,200 thread-count sheets under their bare flesh, like they do in their mansions? Surely one night on a common 500 thread-count sheet isn't enough to ruffle their prim and proper feathers.

This hotel is not the place for the rich; it's for the people like us... the hard up who still want to pay exorbitant prices to slide down a mountain on waxed sticks for a few hours. We need to cut costs somewhere, so why not lay down on strange, dirty beds that still have the stench, body hair and viruses of the last 9,000 people to lay there before us? Because we're not rich in money, we need to be rich in spirit. We laugh at inconveniences like lack of hot water and drafty, ancient windows that cause pneumonia.

My son jumps into the action as well. He snatches my wife's phone and rattles off more depressing reviews.

"The place was dirty and the staff was rude and unprofessional." "It took us forever to check in!"

The list went on and on. I try and seesaw the balance by filtering in the excellent reviews. The kind people that *i've* discovered give 5-stars and say things like "Exceptional" and that is it. These reviews are from mysterious, picture-less people who have given only one review in the 8 years since they joined the site and for some reason felt compelled to give it to this place... an axe murderer's paradise. So now my delicate balancing act of looking at 3-star ratings as more than average might be sliding towards the 2-star mark, and maybe even the 1-½ star mark.

Finally, I had to sit everyone down and have a reasonable chat. I spoke carefully like I would a room full of kindergarteners fearing the boogey man. I presented as exhibit A: Restaurateur and friend Mike Meehan and his wonderful eateries, and how people like to give bad reviews because they're mad and that everyone tends to exaggerate. I let everyone know that a happy and positive attitude would only benefit us.

"We've been through some bad times before, and nothing can shake OUR rock-solid foundations."

After this calm and clear-headed chat, my wife nodded and scooped oatmeal into her mouth and my son smirked and scanned over a Calvin and Hobbes comic. These are the kinds of pep talks you give to people after they've lost everything in a flood, not for people going on vacation! What was happening here? How could this all be so wrong?

I was satisfied that my message was delivered in a rational and dignified manner, but they both knew to expect the worst... and I did too. As long as we got there alive and not on four smoking, fiery wheels, we'd be ok. Everything would work out in the end. If anything, we can laugh about it in years... if not *months* later. My family and friends will shake their heads and say, "Oh A.J., only *you* would do something like this!" Then we'll raise our glasses in a toast to the exterminators who are coming the next day to fumigate our house.

•••

Long gone is our rattling Honda CRV. In August of 2020, my gut instincts kicked in that it was time for a new car. It started in June when the air-conditioner kicked out. June was a sweltering month of nastiness and it was noted by everyone that we needed some cool air moving in the car or a mutiny would surely transpire. I visited my usual mechanic, but he was on vacation for two weeks, so I drove across the street to the adjacent service station.

I was immediately met with the Russian owner who seemed to engage in the transaction like we were dealing plutonium on the black market.

"We can fix it, sure. I don't know. It's up to you."

He shifted in and out of the conversation like one might with bad cell phone reception... except he was standing right before me! I assured him I was there only for the purpose of an AC fix, but he seemed unconvinced.

"You do what you want. You know?"

Perhaps it's hard to take a customer seriously when he's standing before you in bright orange swimming trunks and a 1960s beach boy shirt. If I'd been holding a beer, he may have mistaken me for a man awaiting a hotdog at a bar-b-que. But I was dead set on keeping my family cool on the way to the beach under the unforgiving summer sun. The Russian on the other hand was dressed like a man running an illegal gambling ring in the basement. His mock turtleneck only made him seem overdressed because of the fact it was tucked into his beltless jeans.

I personally diagnosed the AC issue as the car having run out of coolant. Actually, I prayed it was the coolant because it would be the cheapest solution. The Russian took my diagnosis like I'd accused him of money laundering. He held up his hands like a stick-up and cocked his face to the side like it was being pulled by fishing wire.

"I don't know what I'm going to find till I look at the car!" he shouted.

This is the reaction of a man who may have been on trial a few too many times. At this point, his heavy-browed right-hand mechanic sauntered over with an oily rag in hand and buried his face in the engine like he was bobbing for apples.

At this point it was too late. The mechanic was under the engine and yanking out wires. We agreed he'd examine the car for $75 and that he'd call and "let me know." After I walked home, I gave him a call when the phone call he promised me never materialized. He told me the Honda needed a new air compressor and that it would cost $1,000. He said he could put in a used air compressor for $800, but then he couldn't guarantee it. "I don't know, it's up to you. That's *your* decision. You do what you want."

I showed up to the garage on foot, and again, we went through the dance of me not needing any kind of enriched uranium products or contraband of any kind other than a new cooling system for the Honda CRV. His shiftless nature assured me that he was lying through his filthy teeth as I think all mechanics are lying to me. They could tell me I needed a new rotary cuff in my glockenspiel, and I wouldn't know the difference!

The Russian handed me a carbon paper work order, threw his hands up and said, "That's it. That's the price. You do what you want. I don't know." So, I did what I wanted and took the car home and thought about it.

After two days of driving, my good instincts served me well as the Honda began crying out in a terrible moan. I couldn't determine if it was in front of the car or under the car, but it was a noise I'd never heard before. A warbling screech of undetermined material or friction.

I told Rita we needed a new car immediately. This was music to her ears as we'd also recently lost the radio and were forced to listen to CDs mixes I'd made of new wave 80s hits that'd we'd heard so many times, we began to see life as a series of *Breakfast Club* social structures where everyone was classified as either a jock, a stoner, a princess or a nerd.

We decided on a Jeep and called a friend who was a car dealer. He knew a pack of respectable people he'd worked with at the Jeep dealership years ago. "They won't beat you" was his guarantee, and it was good enough for me.

On a sunny Saturday, Rita and I headed to the dealership. As we hooked the CRV onto the highway, the Honda began making the moan again, only this time it began to rise into a frightening level of screaming. The car shook and the steering wheel vibrated to the point that the world outside the windshield came to me in triplicate. The scream eventually hit another level of car ownership terror, making a noise I can only describe as a family of ghosts being dragged on sleds while blowing train conductor whistles.

"Jesus, we're not gonna make it!" I shouted. Rita sank in her seat and prepared herself as though we may fling off the overpass like a loose hubcap. I thought, "Why now?" I was at least hoping to get two grand out of this jalopy. The tree sap coating alone has knocked the value in half... but a lack of A/C and a horrible squeal? They may ask us to pay *them* to take it away.

Fortunately, by the time we'd slowed to a respectable level and entered the dealership parking lot, the Honda buzzed with the timing of a well-wound Swiss watch. Because we were knee deep in the Covid pandemic, the car industry was taking a massive hit, and I was assured by the news, the internet and every boozy grapevine that dealerships were practically giving cars away. The customer would be king, and I could probably bend them over the hood, spread-eagle and take anything I wanted. Especially a fully-stocked car that practically drove itself -- for the low, low price one might pay for a bus ticket.

Upon entering, it was hard to know if anyone could hear anything outside the walls of the place anyway. Especially the moaning Honda. The air was meat-locker cold and the sound system was playing NYC dance club music at ear-splitting decibels. We asked to talk to someone our friend had recommended, and before we knew it, we were kicking the tires of every Jeep on the lot with a woman named Vanessa.

Of course, a customer must give the sense that they are only "looking" and not really in the business of buying... at least, "not today!" Little did Vanessa know that the last thing we planned to do that day was get back into the Honda, which I was convinced was possessed by Russian poltergeists. No sir! We were getting into a Jeep that day, whether we liked it or not.

She asked how much we wanted for the Honda as a trade-in and I stated, quite boldly I might add, that the blue book value was around $9,000 the last time I checked. The last time I checked was 5 years ago, but that was the price. Without so much as an argument, she chirped "OK," like we'd asked her to go for an ice cream. What shocked me more was she was standing right next to the Honda and could clearly see the years of pine tree cum stains that'd dripped over it again and again and again.

After we nodded and rubbed our chins over a series of expensive choices, we settled on a base model black Jeep Cherokee that had not one bell or whistle on it. No seat warmers, no automatic starter... nothing to sparkle the imagination.

Also, nothing that would need servicing in any way, shape or form. It even had a full tank of gas, so that was a plus.

While the paperwork was scratched out, the car was washed and detailed. Vanessa's partner came in and ran my credit, which I believe made a laughing noise. The guy was a huge Hispanic guy named BA and laughed back at my credit score. He assured us that moving some things around and going for more 'high-risk' lenders would do the trick. Lenders who probably take on recent parolee hitmen and Russian mechanic shop owners. Lenders guaranteed to get their return on investment... or else.

Eventually I was approved for a loan and was presented with an itemized list of things that BA explained faster than a Texas cattle auctioneer.

Before I'd arrived that day, I'd planned to go into these transactions with a head full of steam and the fortitude of a thousand forefathers... a refusal to be bilked or fleeced in *any* way. But by the time BA shouted everything I was getting at happy hour levels, my tired, hungry demeanor had crumbled. I nodded like a boxer in the 12th round and simply accepted the information without a fight. The screaming Honda had shaken my nerves and I was unable to regain my footing after that. Any belt adjusting, shoulder-flexing dad vibes I'd hustled into the joint at the beginning, was now a transparent pool of jelly that was dying to get the hell out of there... regardless of the cost.

But it all worked out. I bought the Jeep with almost no money down and with payments sure to keep me in the red for the next seven years. But it came with free oil changes for the life of the car. Sure, I may need to get a second, and maybe even a third job to pay for the thing, but free oil changes twice a year will definitely shave a few bucks off the end cost.

•••

The Jeep is a very pleasant ride. What it has cost me in money has surely been made up for in stress relief. The car runs smooth in all weather and is quieter than a library. The stereo works and the air system springs to life with the gentle touch of an on-screen button. The Honda was a white-knuckle ride that went from zero to 60 in about a day and a half. On the ancient east coast highway entrance ramps, that type of power could get you killed. The Jeep explodes with the tap of the gas and will quickly merge with every lunatic going 30 MPH over the speed limit.

Within minutes of our Vermont journey, we are comfortably tucked into our places for the ride to Stowe. After our first stop, a pee break with a side of donuts and coffee, we're already packed into the vehicle like wine bottles pushed into protective Styrofoam housing. It's been two hours and we're jammed to the gills with hats, gloves, food wrappers, coffee cups, pillows, blankets and papers… all tied together with cell phone charging cables. Every time we leave the car, the seats leave the impressions of garbage snow angels.

We stop for lunch at The Vermont Country Store… A place that I believe was once a quaint country store, but now is a series of shanty town boxes that have been added to each other over time. Selling things like brooms, wooden bowls and other country wares, it also hocks insanely overpriced food items like almond brittle bark, which apparently could

be added to the Dow Jones precious metal index, its value is
so exorbitant.

The road can be a cruel and lonely place, but you
make friends there. Like the red Subaru I followed on I-91 for
an hour. She decided to go 71 miles an hour and that felt like
the perfect speed – exactly 6 MPH over the speed limit. So,
we cruised together... like ducks migrating north. We swept
around slower vehicles using the left passing lane and folded
back into the right lane, using our blinkers. We were in perfect synch, like ice dancers that smoothly released one another
across the rink. But then red Subaru must have gotten distract-
ed and slowed to 62... 3 MPH under the limit. I slowed to 62
and it felt too slow and I got angry! I yelled at Red "What are
you doing?" and jumped in the left lane. Our synchronized
routine had crumbled. I hit the gas and before I knew it, I
had the Jeep bounding at 81, much faster than I wanted to
go. But then Red woke from their slumber and got the 'car
passing secondary vibes.' You know that thing. The sudden
acceleration that a car gets when you try and pass them...
like osmosis, they start to go faster. Suddenly I'm doing 89
MPH because Red has got their piece of shit Subaru up to 81.
If I don't jack the speed to 95, it will take 15 minutes to pass
her. Now we're right next to each other... hurtling down the
highway at death speeds! I'm shouting, "back off!" like I'm in
a war zone. My son yanked his head from his drawing board
and my wife snorted awake. Everyone's in a panic. "What's
going on?" Rita says gripping the door handle. "This mother-
fucker!" I shout and point out the passenger side window. She
looks and expects to see a gangbanger flashing an Uzi, but
it's an old lady with coke-bottle glasses. I gun the Jeep and it

bounds like a lion. I'm pushing 100, and this is the moment where I'm convinced a state trooper is over the next hill with a radar gun. Eventually Red Subaru backs off and, in a few seconds, she's a dot in the rearview. I'm back in the right lane and everyone's pulse has returned to normal. I get sentimental. It was a nice time I had with Red Subaru. We paced and swerved together... laughed at old beater pickup trucks when we passed them... Shook our heads in disappointment at BMWs speeding by us. I eventually attached myself to a dark blue Dodge and together we held steady at 73 as we rolled to the exit ramp.

Eventually, we get to our destination. Google maps tells me so as we roll into the parking lot. Online, the photos show a creepy, yet cheery summer cottage with a crystal blue pool and leafy trees. This place, although not shaded by creepy trees, is a bright, timeworn charmer planted in what I can only identify as ice-cold chocolate mousse. The whole state of Vermont is in a flux of melting and freezing. This "parking lot" is no different. One step can post-hole you in the mud to your knee, while the next step can send your heel skating out from under you. The lot is an expansive pigsty. Patrons have parked wherever they've deemed appropriate and trekked through the muddy mounds to the front door.

Upon entering, beside the standard pamphlet rack showcasing skiers blasting through powdery mounds of snow and recreational hot air ballooning, we're met with couches and chairs that may have been rescued from the American Civil War. Even though everything is burgundy, brown and gold, there's a sheen of beige washed over the place from centuries of wear and tear. The bug-eyed hostess greets us...

her face washed from the blue light of her modern computer check-in system.

"Checking in?" she asks in a half question, half statement kind of way.

She loses her train of thought a few times, then informs us the room is not ready because Marvin is still "mopping the place." My wife nearly curdles at the information.

Rita pictures a school janitor wielding one of those old grey germ mops, loaded with clumps of hair and ball point pen caps as it's dragged across the floor of our room.

I smile, nod and say, "No problem."

You'd like to think when your room is being prepped for occupancy, the end squares of the toilet paper are being folded into triangles and the fluffy white towels are knotted into elephants atop the steam-cleaned bed cover. But I'm certain Marvin's "mop job" will be exemplary. I'm taking all information with gentle ease. Nothing will raise my blood pressure as I've paid too much for this trip. I'm going to be an example of reserve and the center of all reason. She could have stated that Marvin was "removing the corpse from the room" and I would have winked and said, "No rush, we're happy to wait here next to the leather couch where General George Custer bled out."

She hands us the keys and we rescue our suitcases from the car. As we return to the lobby, the hostess asks us again if we're "checking in?" The 30 seconds we were gone completely reset her brain. The realization it was "just us again" sets her off into a bouncing tizzy of laughter usually reserved for clowns sharpening the edge of a machete.

We get to the room and it's a decent enough place to

crash, but my family has a laundry list of infractions that grow with every sniff around every corner. Among the infractions, besides the cleanliness, is the wallpaper. Besides it being endless, it's three creeping walls of green ivy and burgundy... of what can only be described as pornographic illustrations of Audrey II, the monstrous plant from the 1986 film *Little Shop of Horrors*. Audrey II with her toothy mouth agape, Audrey II swallowing a vine connected to another vine, and Audrey II showing us her puckering butthole. All of them serpentining vertically over a geometric beige and white backing pattern that gives the illusion of 3D movement. It's any PTSD sufferer's worst nightmare. While Rita and Max laugh about it, I'm caught into its hypnotic swirl... Audrey II's siren calling me to enter its gangly web and entrap me for a slithering ride.

While they're in the bathroom flipping every wall switch to see what it commands, I find myself on the bed, staring at the ivy walls that support this masterwork of psychedelia.

Rita comes back and snaps me from the funk. "What are doing?"

"checking the bed" I lie as I fold my hands against my chest.

"This place is disgusting" she booms. "There was a big chunk of hair in the corner."

I nod and state that it's only for two nights. Marvin could have waxed the place down to the studs and it wouldn't have been cleaned enough. The online community had poisoned her mind and now every unsightly stain and weird floor discoloration was nothing less than a growing patch of Ebola. Max is also piling on. They wheeled in a metal cot for him to

sleep on which I have absolutely no doubt was used to electro-
cute the mentally disturbed in the late 19th century. It opens
with a clang and squeaks like an attic door. I try it myself and
assure him it's as comfy as a patch of clouds even though it
threatens to snap shut like a bear trap.

We decompress and clear the head before dinner. Max
is on his Nintendo Switch, Rita is on her cell and I'm back
at the wall... Audrey II seductively winking her holes at me
while snaking up and down in squiggles. I'm trying to find the
wallpaper seems where the edges meet, but the job is flawless,
convincing me that the walls are really alive and not paper at
all. The ancient hotel may be falling apart, but somehow, they
got a wallpaper guy with the deft touch of a Beverly Hills
plastic surgeon.

•••

The next day, we're going skiing. We start with the
"Continental breakfast." The night before the hostess said she
"Only charged $2.75 a room for breakfast." It was $2.74 too
much. We woke late so we were left with what can only be
described as scraps. I believe war refugees have had better
meals than what was presented to us as breakfast. Doughy
bagels wrapped in plastic, a tankard of woody coffee and the
remains of cream cheese and other buttery used utensils. Every table has dirty dishes, but a patron says the adjoining room
has tables, so we go in there.

The red-walled room has a massive wooden table surrounded by Winsor chairs and paintings that would normally
have been burned in witch-hunts. I'm pretty sure someone

signed the Declaration of Independence in the place. If someone told me George Washington had been there, I would have
asked "For what? The hotel's 200th anniversary?"

We can barely choke down the food. I go and get nuts
and a granola bar from the room. On my way back, my curi-
osity gets the best of me and I explore.

I turn a corner and discover the room that is advertised on the building's main sign… the Tavern. Again, it is
decorated with things older than time itself, but isn't without
its charm. The glistening bottles set against the mirrored back
wall are catching the early morning sun and the square cut,
unadorned wooden bar is long enough to accommodate an entire crew of stagecoach killers. Its main room is large enough
to have a square dance and feed them all at square tables. I
can see why one reviewer compared it to *The Shining*. Some
of that is due to the swirling, viny red carpeting that coils
through the claustrophobic walls beneath your feet. And there
are ghosts in the place to be sure. Your neck-skin crawls with
their breath. But again, *The Shining* is not the right comparison. Sure, someone has definitely been axed in there before…
probably in the middle of a nice double whiskey. But the bar
in *The Shining* was a swanky establishment where the patrons
wore tuxedos. This is a place where someone was lynched
from the ceiling fan for horse-thieving.

At the mountain, the conditions are Spring-like and
the trails are well groomed. After we park and get our lift tickets, we go through the arduous task of being fitted for equipment. It's like a military drill. March here… march there.
Boots, skis and poles and it's all done with massive amounts

of layered wool clothing, sure to get you drenched in sweat before you get to the top of a frigid mountain whipping with arctic air.

Skiing is not a cheap sport. When my parents took me in my youth, it was more accessible. Renting a place, equipment... even a lift ticket was fairly affordable. Today the cost is out of control. Getting a family of four on the mountain will cost you an arm and a leg. Literally! It's hard to ski with one arm and one leg. You can do it, but to have all four limbs is preferential. The cost of lunch at the mountain lodge can decrease your credit rating. The prices are not movie theater popcorn levels of absurdity... but it's pretty close!

We do a few bunny hill runs to warm up. Well, Max and I do... while Rita watches. My wife was born and raised in a country where the only snow she saw was on TV. Walking on snow is still a challenge for her, so encasing her feet in brick-like boots and slapping slippery sticks to the bottom of them is a recipe for disaster.

On her first run she falls eight times. The hill is about 25 yards long, so it equates to a fall every three feet or so. I try to calmly instruct her, but by the second run I'm barking ridiculous commands like "Feel it out!" and "Control the skis, don't let them control you!"

After an hour and a half, I'm sweating and exhausted and she's completely dejected. In the final run, she plowed into a 3-year-old child, crumpled into a heap, and flopped into a snow embankment for a five-minute rest. I knew deep in my soul that it would be easier to teach a fish to ride a bicycle than to teach Rita to ski. It was as if I'd cemented her hands and feet in blocks and asked her to wrangle a greased pig. She couldn't do it, so she released Max and I to explore higher grounds on our own.

Max's main concern isn't going down the mountain, but going up the mountain. He's afraid of heights and is worried the chair lift will toss him to the side in a clump of embarrassment. But the four-person lift scoops us up with ease and we're in the air without a fall.

A chairlift is a place of Zen. You catch angles of the mountain you can't see otherwise... an extra summit, a small valley and an inspirational vista. We catch a ride with a toddler in ski school, then later, an old man with his grandchild.

When I was a kid, we loved getting on the chairlift with strangers. It was the best place to practice your bold-faced lies. My sister and our friends would tell the biggest whoppers we could imagine to people gullible enough to believe them. We'd bend the ear of a couple from Utah to invoke sympathy after we told them our house burned to the ground just a few weeks ago. "But here we are! Swooshing down the mountain without a care in the world!" We'd tell people our parents died in a plane crash, that I was shot in the eye with a gun and had a fake eye... "I don't see as well, obviously, but it doesn't stop me from skiing." We'd have a captive audience on the chairlift. My buddy Brad or my friend Chip would suddenly be my half-brother. "We have the same mom, but our sisters have three dads!" It was like an improv acting troop. My cousin Christen, my sister Caroline, me and a friend would get on the singles line and merge into an unsuspecting chair threesome. Our audiences would hear tales of piracy, orphanages and world treks that would make Marco Polo jealous. My family improv group would wait at the top for me and hear my chair-mates sing "Auf Wiedersehen, Ralph... hope you get that liver donor!" as I swooshed away. I'd wave goodbye enthusiastically to the group of Swedes I'd just met, like I was off to new adventures on a steam ship to Africa. As our group reconvened, we compared notes. My sister was my mother, Christen was a British ex-pat, and Brad was adopted by my parents, who found him on their doorstep in a wicker basket.

It's a grand day at the mountain. Max and I don't tell any tall tales, but we do as many runs as we can, while Rita does cross-country around the lodge. Rita can now walk in ski boots like a champ and she's able to carry her equipment without hitting small children across the face.

Grey clouds roll in and the rain comes down. Vermont, which was a firm, yet icy-coated bowl of chocolate pudding, devolves into an unruly kettle of beef stew. Every step is a swampy challenge.

Every understaffed restaurant we entered was overwhelmed by hungry people. Up until that point, according to my family, we'd failed to eat a decent meal. Our meals have been... under-cooked, underwhelming, not what was expected and not cut out for war-torn refugees. Last night's dinner was blackened... and not in the recipe's 'Cajun style' but in the 'left over the fire too long' style. But we snuck into every restaurant early and were seated in good time. Every complaint by the family is met with my calm demeanor and some form of dad philosophy like "tomorrow's another day" or "I'm sure it's grade A beef and not moose meat." Some of that is fueled by tequila and the fact that I will eat just about anything... whether it's raw, burnt or somewhere in the middle. But mainly I'm trying to enjoy myself and remain a pillar of reason in an otherwise chaotic and depressing world. I'm always prepared to roll out the whole "People are dying in the streets and you're complaining about a poorly-seasoned chicken leg!" argument. But my wife and son work as hard as me in their respective worlds and deserve well-cooked chicken and streets unencumbered by mudslides. So, they can be free to say what they want, knowing full well that I can, and will order another margarita and if necessary, eat two ice creams if that's what it takes to reach a place of mental peace.

•••

At check out, we approach the desk with our key. The desk woman is different this time. We've seen her lingering about the place in the background shadows... teetering in the back room with the copier machine and standing in the corner with the vending machine that is glowing, but completely empty of snacks. Her head is shaped like a pear, which is buried into the shoulders of her body, which is also shaped like a pear. She's wearing a flowered mumu of sorts, and could blend into a set of window curtains with relative ease. I show her the key and put it on the counter.

"We're checking out" I ring with glee. "Room 210!"

Although the woman is smiling widely at me and nodding, her bugged eyes are staring to her left towards the ground. It's as awkward as an interaction gets. I slide the key a touch closer and sing "bye" as to invoke perhaps a simple 'goodbye' or 'thank you' from her. Unfortunately, her gaze does not break from the floor, nor does she conjure any sound from her throat, but her head continues its monotonous, calculated nod. I'm convinced this woman has tasted human blood not of her own and spent time in some sort of institution for the criminally insane... but I'm not one to judge.

A storm is brewing and we're forced out of Vermont a day early. At my cousin Lauren's, we snow shoe and tap a few maple trees in hopes that in a few months, the sap will flow and be cooked into the sweet nectar called maple syrup. Justin sends us off with a bottle after feeding us well. Their AirBNB is cozy, but a blizzard is coming and we need to shove off. We love the Jeep, but we don't want to sleep in it during zero-degree weather. I've seen enough stories on CNN where an innocent family loses their way during a whiteout and then next thing you know, it's a gruesome tale about a family that trekked from their car to find help and became lost and turned to cannibalism. A reporter will note how it's even more tragic as the family was found about 50 yards from the back of a 7/11 and if they'd walked just a bit further, they could have eaten foot-long hot dogs instead of each other.

We press our bodies into the car garbage and fill the gas tank. We're on the road again and heading south. Our final meal was one I cooked... bacon and pancakes. After it's been digested, Rita asks Max if he had a good time and he responds enthusiastically that he did! Rita agrees it was a great time.

My eyes widen like saucers. I'm pretty sure I heard nothing but grim details about every aspect of the trip... from ancient furniture, to bad food, to rotten weather conditions. Even the stores offered no glimmer of hope for a purchase. But apparently it was all love and good vibes. Maybe they have terrible memories as we'd only just left the place a few hours ago. Perhaps in our desire to get to the joy, we realized the joy was in the getting to the joy.

When I eat an ice cream bar, sometimes I feel the need to tolerate the chocolate coating around the creamy ice cream, but then you realize the chocolate is really good, and if eaten with the ice cream it makes for a good taste combination. Maybe our evisceration of the Axe Murder Inn was part of the fun. Maybe the blackened burger and charred fish was more memorable than the well-seasoned chicken. Maybe mud can leave an impression as deep as a footprint in the snow. Where else can you spend 8 quality hours with your family than in the car during a hellish bout of inching traffic?

Max notes that I said George Washington is probably hanging on the wall somewhere in the hotel. I don't even remember saying that! But Rita assures me that she'll be choosing the hotel next vacation, which means I'll be getting another job to pay for it. She definitely won't be choosing the $200 deal buster that I found. She'll find the $1,400 beachfront hut that costs more than college tuition. There won't be an axe murder anywhere near the place. The only edged weapon in the vicinity will be a knife used to carve fruit so it can be tossed into blenders. We're pretty sure the next winter trip will be in Florida, which is fine by me. We can drive there and forgo plane tickets and airports. I smile and nod. I think that's a good plan. Florida in winter is a fine place to be. I can feel the sun and taste the margaritas already.

My mind begins to wander as I emotionally latch onto a blue Subaru that is cruising at a comfortable 73 MPH in front of me. She signals well before a lane change and returns swiftly to the right lane after being a safe distance from the car she passed.

Once we're settled into our comfy Long Island home, I sip some wine and get on the computer. We contemplate leaving a review for the Axe Murder Inn. My wife wants to give it Zero-stars, saying...

"Gross. If you're 2 or 3 young guys, it's ok for a day or two, but for a family... no way!"

My son at first gives it Negative 5-stars, then in a stunning reversal, gives it 3-stars.

"The place is dirty, but comfortable."

Opening my email, I see my cousin has left me an exalted AirBNB review. 5-stars! Apparently, we're the shining example of renters. No bias at all! We didn't puke in the closet or shit in the sink or anything like that. We're civilized. I, in turn, give them a rave review. 5-Stars! I mention the cleanliness, the coziness and the convenience as well as the maple syrup. This is how online reviews should work. If we're blessed enough to afford to get away in these horrible economic times we live in, then tell your host what a wonderful time you had, even if a few hiccups occurred along the way. My cousin's rental is a quaint little place that is exactly what you want from a Vermont getaway... charm, comfort, wilderness... and nary an axe murder in sight.

At least I don't think there were any axe murders around. You never know. I don't think my cousins are axe murderers. I didn't even see an axe on the premises. They don't look like axe murderers. But, I suppose you don't really know people deep down inside... do you?

HOL-I-DAY EQUAL-I-TAY

America is a melting pot! You hear that term a lot, don't you? We're a melting pot! And for the most part it's true. And not because we melt cheese in a pot and dip our chips inside. Although we do that too. We're a melting pot because we have different cultures, religions and races from all over the world living in this great country of ours. It's what makes America... AMERICA!

But we're not necessarily a melting pot when it comes to our religious celebration breaks. The holiday calendar and the times in which our children get off from school, and adults off from work, is still centered around the Christian calendar. Christmas and the Christian holidays rule the timeframe in which we enjoy a long weekend. And I guess that's fine as long as everyone is cool with that. Is everyone cool with that? I know over the last few years we've made more concessions in our work and school breaks for Jewish holidays. But I'm not sure we cut back in other areas. It seems like my son has

THE DEATH OF OUR DREAMS

about two months off at Christmas time and then again for Spring break and then Easter break and then some other kind of break, and then the whole summer off. Do kids go to school anymore? When I was in school, I went to school every day, 13 months a year for 27 years. Is it any wonder our country is 39th in education out of all the industrialized nations on Earth? Did I just pull that number out of my ass?

Yes!

But this isn't about our terrible education system. It's about how we divide our time between all the religions. Being the lazy agnostic/Catholic that I am, I have no clue as to when any of the Islamic holidays are and how long they would celebrate them for. I know Ramadan is a really long holiday and we can't take a month off to celebrate it, but can't we squeeze in a few days off for it? I think so. Considering a billion people celebrate it, it might be time to recognize it. As someone whose family is Catholic, I'm more than willing to give up Easter so that someone can have the time to do something. Don't the Hindus have a say in this?

Maybe it's time for all the religions to pick one holiday in which we ALL take some time off and we move on from there. Start staking some calendar tent poles. Why do we have so many calendars? Can't we have just one calendar? Is it really necessary to have so many different new years' celebrations? Can we agree to have just one? I know the Chinese have a great New Year. Maybe we can celebrate that one. I happen to like the color red, dragons, Chinese food and Chinese people, so maybe I'm biased. I'm not crazy about firecrackers though. Have you ever seen how much Chinese people can drink? They can drink like fish. I go to my local

Chinese place and order take out and I leave shit-faced. They order tequila shots and refuse to let me go until I'm cross-eyed drunk. Damn fine people. Now I'm convinced we need to eliminate all New Years' celebrations and only do the Chinese New Year.

Most of us are just thankful to have some time off. Would you really care if you got a few days off for Ramadan? Of course not! I'd be totally psyched! If someone said, "hey, want a four day weekend?" I'd say, "Yes, please!" I may be a tad jaded here, but we're not jumping for joy because we have time off to worship, we're jumping for joy because we have a few days reprieve from our stupid bosses, lazy co-workers and generally monotonous work lives.

But there's only 365 days in the year and we do need to get some work done, so that's why we need to start staking some tent poles now. People don't like change, but we need to rework the holiday calendar a bit.

We'll keep Thanksgiving, of course. That's the warm-hearted American holiday when we killed off the Native Americans. So that's an automatic tent pole right there. I'm being sarcastic, of course—I truly love Thanksgiving and it's a day that is all about family and nothing more. It's also about food too. I love stuffing and whenever we eat it I say "Why don't we eat stuffing more often?" then I never do. It's like when I get a massage and say "Man, I'm going to get a massage every week" then three years goes by until I get another massage.

Memorial Day is an essential holiday in giving a hearty thanks to our dead war vets. Labor Day is a particular favorite of mine as it's a day in which we do no labor at all.

It should be called No Labor Day, but hey, it's time off from work no matter how you slice it. We have the all-important Fourth of July to celebrate the founding of our nation, but after that everything is up for grabs in my opinion. These three summer holidays involve a smoking grill and that's one of my favorite places to be besides a warm shower and bed. If I'm near a grill, I know I'll be eating something tasty, I'll be warm and most likely drinking a cool, fermented beverage.

Christmas is a HUGE tent pole. That will never change because our economy basically rotates around this cash-cow holiday. I love Christmas. My family loves Christmas because they get lots of good stuff. I don't want anything. I love Christmas because I really love... Christmas music. Weird, I know. Christmas music makes me delirious with joy, which you won't hear me say very often. I love all the 'I'll be by the fire' and 'chestnuts on my nose' and all the other classics. There's about 8,922,367 different Christmas songs and I've heard them all. Give or take 33,412. I'll even listen to Christmas music in summer if it happens to hit the rotation on my iPhone.

Perhaps if holidays like Diwali and the Buddhist celebration of Vesak had a chance to be woven more into the fabric of our society, there'd be more songs about them. Michael Bublé could release an album every month of chart-topping classics like "I'm Chipper for Yom Kippur" "Ramadan-a-ding-dong" and of course the Holi day classic "colored powder gets in your eyes" as well as many other toe-tapping selections. Talk about an untapped market. I can smell the dollar signs already.

But we get big hunks of time off for the Christmas

holiday and it's only fair that other religions get time off for their holidays too. Unfortunately, these holidays may not come at the most convenient times. If they're all crammed in at the same timeframe, we may have to close the country for two months while we drink and/or fast ourselves into a religious stupor. Someone may have to make some sacrifices and it may not be pretty. Some holidays are really not worth celebrating. Any Jew worth his salt will pretty much tell you that Hanukkah is a nothing holiday that got trumped up so their children had something to celebrate while their bratty friends got heaps of Christmas gifts. So maybe they agree for no time off for Hanukkah. I'm just throwing out ideas here—don't get upset.

Yom Kippur bounces around the calendar a bit, so perhaps the Jews take Yom Kippur as their big holiday, keep a consistent date and take a week off for that at the end of September. I know, I know. There's probably some kind of God frowning down upon me right now, but we must make sacrifices, right? Isn't that what Yom Kippur is all about? Sacrifices? …I think? ….Anyone?

So, let's have a review. Here's how I think things could work out if we keep an open mind. Let's have Yom Kippur around, let's say September 20th-ish, Navariti (Hindu festival of worship) around October 15th-ish, we can keep Thanksgiving where it is and then Christmas on December 25th. That's a good start! Then we celebrate the Chinese New Year and forget all these freakin' famous birthdays and bust our asses straight through till about April where we can celebrate Ramadan around April 15th-ish. And don't get me started on Scientology. That's a whole different subject in itself.

Once we get the big holidays locked up, we can work on the smaller ones. Trust me, no one in my family is going to cry if we don't have off for Easter, but I can tell you now that I'd really look forward to having a few days off in August, and then September, and then October, and then November and then end the year with big ol' chunk of Christmas/New Years break and start the new year off refreshed.

Maybe we can start making up some new holidays— not just celebrating the same old holidays. That seems very American and democratic. Maybe we can have a committee and see if we can get a round table discussion about coming up with a new holiday. How does God Day sound? Or maybe, Holy Worship Day? I don't know. I'm just throwing out ideas. As long as I have a three-day weekend, I don't really give a crap.

GOVERNMENT CHEESE

There are three subjects you should never talk about in mixed company and they're money, religion and politics. Why? Because you're bound to butt heads with someone whose opinion differs wildly from your own and that is never a pretty thing. Especially when it's about subjects that are as polarizing as money, religion and politics.

The same can be said for writing about these three subjects as well. Unfortunately, I already broke those rules by writing about money and religion in the early part of this book. Most of my thoughts about money are universal, and I didn't stand behind any secular standpoint; just that we need to open the American holiday calendar for different religions to worship besides the Christians. Basically, it was a selfish plea to get more days off from work. And you can't really argue with that logic.

But now I'm about to open another can of worms and write about politics. Although I won't say anything that you don't already know. I'm a registered Independent myself, back when it meant that I didn't want to be a part of any particular party because I always wanted to vote for the best candidate no matter what their affiliation was and I think the party system is destroying the government from within.

I'm not the only one who thinks that. In fact, George Washington, Alexander Hamilton, and John Adams were vehemently against the two-party system because they thought it would divide the country. Thomas Jefferson and James Madison wanted a two-party system to prevent Washington from turning the country into a monarchy. Basically. It goes much deeper, but I won't bore you with details.

All you should know is that the two parties (the Federalists & the Democrats) have been butting heads ever since. Except now the Federalists are the Democratic Party and the Democrats are the Republicans. I know, it's confusing. If you want to know more, crack open your kid's American History text book. Now the Independents are an actual party and have been nothing more than a mosquito-like nuisance since the day they came to be.

Anyway, unless you've been living under a piece of plywood in the woods (the one with spiders and pill bugs attached to it) then you know that the fires of the Presidential furnace are always being stoked. If you didn't realize that a Presidential election is coming, I completely understand. That's because there's *always* a presidential election coming up. As soon as one guy gets in, the other party is plotting to get him out. God help us all.

That means we're about to be subjected to an onslaught of mudslinging and name calling campaigns, the likes of which we've never seen. And it will go on and on for years. Simply dreadful.

Remember in the *Lord Of The Rings* films when the Mountains of Mordor started heating up? Enormous trees were chopped down and tossed into giant fires and orcs were digging other orcs out of the muddy ground, forming an army to do battle on Middle Earth. This parable is completely relevant to the Presidential Election. The only difference is that the battles will take place on TV and the orcs are in suits—their weapons are words, and their shields are polished with Crest White Strips and Brylcreem.

This is the main reason you're always seeing a bunch of sharp dressed people on the news—because of this "upcoming" election. You've seen them, of course. They look like a culmination of people you've totally despised throughout your life—pushy teachers, incompetent bosses, aggressive Wall Street douchebag types and every other self-important, moneyed mannequin-like humanoid who are completely and utterly out of touch with what is actually going on in the world outside of their stock portfolio and their powerful friends' self-interests. They're cocked, loaded and ready to go—their sites aimed clearly at our current President. And I'm not just talking about the other party. Everyone is gunning for the Big Guy.

The current president usually hasn't done anything to show he's ready for the barrage of bombs that are coming his way. He's stuck in a quagmire of problems the last guy left so he's desperately trying to dig out of that pile of shit, while trying to employ millions of unemployed people, by creating jobs that don't exist, for services that no one needs or wants.

It's a lose-lose situation and no one in his ranks is competent enough to tell him otherwise.

I worked in politics for a year as the Creative Director of a political PR firm. It was by far, the most depressed I've ever been at a job. I liked the company, I liked my work mates… it's just that I became supremely aware of how the sausage was made and after that, I didn't want to grill anymore. Not that I could grill anyway as the political machines run in the summertime and while everyone I knew was traipsing off to the beach, I was slumped in front of a computer in an ice-cold office creating campaigns for people who I'm almost positive couldn't tie their own shoes. It makes you lose faith in the system. You start to wonder what other systems are teetering on the brink of ruin and you realize *all* of them are.

It's a fragile world we live in!

There's always a battle to be won in politics. It happens on the local level too… mayors, judges, sheriffs, congresspeople. The small battles reverberate through the spine of the political nervous system as much as the big ones. When the president is Democrat, the Republicans fight all the little battles around the country to get the momentum moving so they can slowly tip the rock over the summit so it roles in their favor. Think globally, act locally applies to politics as much as anything.

One memorable campaign we ran, we had a 50-year-old lawyer who sent out so many mailers in so many languages over the course of two months, it may have been easier to fly a plane over the area and drop pamphlets like snow. Like a World War II propaganda dump. After spending an absurd amount of money, he lost to a girl practically out of college who sent out two mailers a week before the election.

In upstate New York, the Republicans completely re-drew the district voting lines so that a slick corporate shark was guaranteed to win. The Democrats tossed out a dairy farmer as the candidate whose eastern European last name was so complicated, you would have thought someone mashed their fists into a keyboard to write it. We sent mailers with her name spelled phonetically so people could pronounce it.

She won. So, you never know how the political voting tables will turn.

Our two-party government works on a pattern that hasn't changed in a hundred years or so— The Republicans come into power, get all their rich friends even richer, while raising the national debt and walk all over the common people, while simultaneously blowing the holy bejesus out of some remote country 9,000 miles away from the comfy confines of Washington D.C. Then, the Democrats come in and clean some of this shit up. They shake a few hands overseas... say sorry. Promise not to raise taxes, then raise taxes to insane heights and distribute all the money in a socialist fashion that makes the words 'fiscal responsibility' seem like a magical thing that no one has seen... like a unicorn. The Independents have no power because they're in the middle. They tend to be the party that both the Republicans and the Democrats want to sway. So instead of being centrists who can take the best parts of both parties and apply them to a philosophy, they are simply pawns that get advertised to twice as much.

Our government is a giant business. Maybe the most profitable business in the history of the world. That's the way our politicians run it. Our stock portfolio is built on guns, war and oil. Special interest groups have a firm grip on the testicles of our politicians... even the females. They're yanking their scrotums around like dog leashes, getting our leaders to vote on their private interests with every tug and jerk. Lobbyists dangle money in front of our elected officials like a carrot on a stick. There's no real political work happening at all.

Our politicians don't understand that the purpose of being an elected official is to serve the public. Most think it's an opportunity to line their pockets. So doing things like stopping the slaughter of our children and enacting gun policies is ignored. It's bad business. It's a money decision. Things like gun control, feeding the hungry and housing the homeless is a money-losing proposition, so we don't do it. Government is as cutthroat and dumb as any business. Our senators are drones and our president is usually as misinformed as any president whether it's the president of the free world or the president of a burger joint.

Fortunately, most, if not all, of our presidents have been complete and total characters.

The last president to have almost no real impact on the social fabric of the country was Jimmy Carter. Other than having a giant set of choppers, he was more or less wallpaper. He enjoyed peanuts and having people walk over him like a carpet.

Then former actor Ronald Reagan moseyed in, with his slicked back hair and Alzheimer's shake. He changed the world as we know it. And not always for the better. He built up our military, gutted the EPA and ignored AIDS till it spread across the entire planet.

Then his Vice President won a term... a guy who was

the living incarnation of the Snow Miser from the holiday special *A Year Without A Santa Claus*. George HW Bush came in and said something about "no new taxes," then made new taxes. He also said something about trickle-down economics, which 35 years later we're still waiting to trickle down.

Then we got our biggest character yet... Bill Clinton. Somehow this pussy hound stayed in office for 8 years even though he was banging everything that moved -- except his wife Hillary. Who would have thought that a guy with a dick for a nose would like to chase tail and bang women at every opportunity? Slick Willy was using the Oval Office as his own personal bang palace, which is unfortunate because you'd hope something like the prestigious Oval Office would be exempt from that type of thing. Although I'm sure John F. Kennedy banged Marilyn Monroe in there, so Bill wasn't the first. Richard Nixon, who also had a dick for a nose, and his name was actually Dick, fucked the entire country over in the Oval Office, so I guess maybe it's a traditional fuck palace after all.

After that, we got HW's kid, George W. Bush. Former coke fiend party animal and all-around clueless monkey, *Dubya* let his vice president Dick Cheney do all the work while he did a bunch of other stuff. What that stuff was, we're not sure.

Then we got another 8 year candidate, Mr. Barrack Obama. That was a game changer to be sure, whether you voted for him or not. First black president. A great orator and charmer, he did his best. Unfortunately, he pretty much disappeared in his last three years as the head honcho.

"Where's Barrack? Oh well, we'll let the country run itself until someone else is elected!"

Then we got the orange crush -- white nationalist Donald Trump. Why anyone thought a sexist, spoiled brat Nazi and so-called 'billionaire' who is more detached than anyone about what people need would make a good president is beyond me, but he got in there and proceeded to shit the bed.

Trump was so obnoxious that everyone willed Joe Biden into office, even though I think Joe Biden died in 2017. I'm almost positive we have a *Weekend at Bernie's* situation happening with Joe. If you've never seen that masterpiece of a film, that's the one where two guys carry their dead boss around for a weekend so they can avoid... ah, who gives a shit. It's an 80s classic regardless. Stream it.

Anyway, Joe Biden is being pushed from podium to podium while wires and puppetry are used to manipulate his face. We're already talking about getting him the hell out of there.

So here we are... again. Interviewing obnoxious political candidates for a chance to win the job as president of these here United States of America. They're going to smile and say all sorts of bullshit that they think we want to hear, make promises they can never keep and make wild claims we can never cross reference to see if they're true.

We're still in the stages of elimination. Sort of like a reality game show where candidates try and knock the other candidates out of the competition. Like the show Survivor, except these people actually influence your life in some way— frightening!

When all is said and done, we'll have two (or three) candidates, both (or all) of whom have displayed every horrible character flaw known to man, and it will be left in our capable hands to decide which is the lesser of two (or maybe three) evils.

The focus will get super tight and then we can dissect each candidate and their own personal history with laser like precision; like a corpse on CSI. It's going to be exhausting.

We the people have to decide which mouth-frothing lunatic, who just spent a year assassinating the character of everyone except their own family, will be running the country. It's going to get racial, it's going to get ugly and it's going to get downright nasty.

Good Luck!

You're going to need it...

NIGHT WIGGA

I used to work with a guy named Topper Rimel – a smooth guy with a breezy disposition. He was kind of like Pee Wee Herman on a handful of sedatives. We became fast friends. He was from La Jolla, California… that's in San Diego if you didn't know. A beautiful place. Stunning, really. Step onto the flat, unbroken shores where the water gently varnishes over the sand and you fall under the spell of an ethereal massage. The water, sun and air are all at the right temperatures and in the right proportions.

Topper was the bass player in a band called *The Origin*, which had about 5 seconds of alternate rock success in the early 90s. For some reason, Topper hopped on a plane and planted roots in New York and became a designer. We met designing toys in the cold, hard offices of Manhattan… fourth floor… corner of 17th Street and 5th Avenue.

Thieves had broken into the office and snatched the computers so many times, it forced us to move our Macs into a 15 x 20 reinforced back room. Four designers crammed daily into a dark space with barred windows and a gated entryway was akin to a prison cell... about as far away as you can get from playing bass guitar on the warm, sandy beaches of southern California.

In early summer of 2001, Topper invited me to a rooftop birthday party in the West Village. It may have been his own birthday party, I'm not sure. I arrived at an industrial apartment building on a bland stretch of street and pressed a door button. Eventually, someone buzzed me in. I got to the top floor and approached a door that was ajar. I pushed it open and found people milling about in a kitchen where they clanged ice in their drinks and passed my view in a blur. It was a functioning chef's kitchen, except these people were drunk and styled to be at a chic summer party.

I placed the six-pack of beer I'd brought as a token of entry on the counter and wandered to a staircase that guided me to the roof.

It was a gorgeous day, with a perfect view of upper Manhattan. The Empire State Building twinkled in the afternoon light as the heat beat down on our backs -- the sweet summer air wafted off the Hudson in tingling waves of refreshment. Every rooftop garden, on every column of brick building could be seen sprouting it's leafy fruits like a valley of fingering stalagmites... their vegetative tips in row after row of budding herbs, hanging gardens, pergolas, canopies and flourishing trees. The real life of the city... the escapes up top... away from the hustling, bustling streets where chewing gum and honking cabs bubbled on the hot tar of the urban jungle.

I fished my arm into a cooler of ice, came up with a beer, and before I knew it, I was sitting behind a makeshift drum set... which I'd been known to do from time to time. Cobbled together almost as an afterthought, the drum kit had a high-hat, snare, ride cymbal and a kick drum that consisted of a foot peddle set to hammer into a dull cardboard box.

Topper played bass and a guy named Steve de Seve played guitar. Steve was Greek, or Spanish... or perhaps Portuguese... with his dark curly hair, hooked nose and tan, Mediterranean skin tone. He had dark, lidded eyes and was the kind of guy who had five O'clock shadow by two in the afternoon. The three of us stumbled like amateurs through a variety of classic rock hits that most people turn off when they hear them on the radio so they can listen to better music.

After the set, which consisted of early Beatles and other easy-to-play bubble gum classics, Steve beamed and said "That was awesome" even though I'm positive the audience wanted us to stop playing at least half an hour before we did. Steve wanted to form a band, which seemed like a revolutionary idea after I'd consumed more beer than I'd lost in sweat. Steve felt I had the chops to form the backbone of a band even though my talent was one step up from one of those obnoxious bug-eyed, cymbal-crashing chimp toys. We exchanged emails and partied deep into the summer night.

Over the years I'd been in a few bands. The last one, aptly named The Last Hombres, was a band fronted by my uncle Paul. I was kicked out of that band because not only did I frequently miss practices, I was not a particularly good drummer. I was eventually replaced by someone more competent... Levon Helm. The drummer in *The* Band... who played with Bob Dylan, who played at Woodstock, and sang such classic hits as *The Weight* and *Up On Cripple Creak*. So needless to say, a vast improvement over me.

The following Monday, I was back at work but Topper was not. He escaped the comfy confines of our cold metal cell to design handbags at a new gig in midtown. He also seemed to break out on the notion of joining the band, which left Steve and I to round out the overall structure. Almost immediately Steve sent me emails containing Fela Kuti music and an MP3 of someone singing over a drum machine. Upon first listening to the MP3, I thought, "Who is this maniac?" Then I realized it was him. Steve, who bore a wonderful, timber-filled voice, howled some kind of African accent over a sparse drum machine whose sound quality and accompanying pre-programmed percussion features couldn't have been more sophisticated than a kid's Casio keyboard.

After the first listen of Steve's rendition of *Use Me* by Bill Withers, I couldn't quite grasp what was happening. It's one of those moments when you're unsure if you're being led into a den of stupid or hopping on a magic carpet ride to pure genius. As open as I was to any thought, idea, or adventure, I couldn't quite grasp what was truly happening or how I would fully make this abstract idea work. Then after a few more ingestions of Fela Kuti's *Shuffering and Shmilling*, a light bulb went off. Steve wanted to do Nigerian Afrofunk music, but to American songs. After I listened to him sing a few more times on that MP3, I realized that there was something amazing happening. I followed my instincts and punched my ticket to the show. My instincts are either dead-on or wildly off... there's no middle ground. I knew either way it was going to be totally amazing or a shit-show.

That Wednesday night, I dragged my bongos and a floor conga from my Manhattan apartment onto the 6 train, and then caught a 4 train which dropped me off at Borough Hall in Brooklyn, a few streets over from Steve's apartment.

The life of a drummer is not an easy one. Not only do they carry about 10 times more equipment than their band-mates, but the spontaneity level drops when someone wants to jam in a random place. A guitarist can pull out an acoustic and sing around a campfire or under a tree. Drummers, un-less they have a small travel bongo set, must lug countless chromed-coated poles, hard edged cymbals and cases filled with heavy, unruly equipment which will surely break your back at some point in your life. Unless you get famous and hire eager, young men to lug the shit around for you... which was a luxury I didn't have. Fortunately, I'd sold my drum set to my friend Chip, who proceeded to bang the thing to pieces, while I escaped with my marginally tighter setup of bongos, congas and tambourines... which stacked neatly onto one sturdy, retractable stand.

Steve's apartment was a long railroad with multiple rooms that housed many roommates who all seemed to be recruited into the band either with complete and total devo-tion to the act, or rather reluctantly because they happened to be in the vicinity and they said yes. The ramshackle place was stuffed with things... makeshift beds, vintage side tables, boxes of stuff, papers, art supplies, musical equipment and

an array of mismatched chairs and stools. It was as if someone took an entire garage sale and stuck it in an apartment in
Brooklyn.

Steve cooked everyone a chicken dinner with a
healthy side of beer and marijuana, which served as a week-
ly routine. While Steve downloaded every Fela Kuti album
he could off of Napster, we formed some of our early hits...
Life in the Vaseline (Life in the Fast Lane), Layla and Magic
Man. The downstairs neighbor would bang on her ceiling for
us to shut up and we'd shout at her through the floor that we'd
"only be another hour or two."

The band at its earliest incarnation was me, Steve,
multi-instrumentalist Gavin -- a very gifted keyboard player
who'd also jump on the sax; Mike, Steve's roommate who'd
do random percussion; Alex the guitarist and Casey, our only
backup singer. Steve would man and 'play' a base machine
that would thump the room and keep a lowdown, on-the-one
beat.

Playing under the working title Night Ranger (even
though we knew there was a classic rock band with that name
already) we settled on doing classic rock covers to Nigerian
funk music. We donned ourselves from head to toe in random
costumes, wore strange wigs that we most likely had from
past Halloweens, and hid behind sunglasses to protect our
identities from any potential cannon fodder.

We did a few random shows around Brooklyn that
were more like drunken mash-fests as we weren't completely
sold on the concept ourselves just yet.

We figured if we were out for the night, might as well
get shit-faced drunk and have a good time... even though we

needed to be on stage. But, something magical happened on the way to the party. We started to get good.

Besides being our front man, Steve was in a constant state of band recruitment. While out watching other shows -- any jazz trumpeter, any coffeehouse guitarist, any random percussionist he saw standing even a fraction away from the rest of his band-mates would get Steve in their ear for an open invitation to join our band. Many who came to our practices would be horrified at the unprofessionalism and never be seen again. Some would come and do a few shows and then go MIA. Some lingered around for months before they drifted away. I never caught any of their names and if I did, I've forgotten them by now.

Almost immediately, the six core members were joined by two friends, Christine and Abby, who saw us at a show. Christine and Abby brought incredible dynamics to the band. Much like the backup singers to Bob Marley, The Wailers, the girls brought a range to the band we'd been lacking before. Besides good harmonies, they added a call and response to some songs that the audience would shout along to.

Abby was a short, curvy, sandy-haired sparkplug with a cheerleader body who could dance like no one I've ever seen. Christine was a pale, raven-haired waif with big blue eyes with an ornate star tattoo around her navel. The girls dressed sexily and practiced and executed dance routines to accompany their singing.

The Band would fluctuate in size over time. Some nights we'd have anywhere from 10 to 11 people performing

on stage and as few as six. At full strength, our band consisted of three horns, three backup singers, two percussionists,
Steve, Alex and Gavin. When in full head-bouncing groove,
we could reach the stratospheric heights of any band in New
York City... and when off, sounded like a garbage truck
crushing a barrel of tuneless bagpipes.

A friend and fan of the band stitched us all genuine
costumes from scratch, each with our own African pattern
and accompanying hat. Mine was black with orange, mus-
tardy leaves that perfectly suited my blonde, brown-eyed coloring... capped off with a grey bowler hat. Considering we
were all white except for Casey, who was a mix of black and
Hispanic, we were treading heavily on cultural appropriation.
With our newly minted costumes and flowing wigs, we magically transported into Night Wigga, because... we wore wigs.
But after gaining a modicum of success, it was pointed out
that if we switched the first two letters of each name, you'd
get White Nigga, which completely shocked us even though it
was staring us dumbly in the face the whole time. This caused
a stir. Some outsiders felt we were being insensitive. But Casey defended our band name choice and we marched on as
Night Wigga, and with us... a small, but loyal following.

•••

Our first major gig was a showcase of hot bands in
New York that were to take the stage at a small venue near
City Hall called Tribeca Blues. We were the last act on the
bill, which started early for a Saturday night – 7:00pm. The
place was jammed, and the acts ranged from country to hard

core rock and the packed crowd sweated to the sounds of music, shoulder-to-shoulder in the warm Summer night.

By the time we took the stage at 11:00, the place had pretty much cleared out, leaving about 25 stragglers who were worn and drunk as sailors. One guy was so bombed, he was splayed back in his chair at a center stage table, head back, mouth agape and snoring. It seemed the other acts had rocked the place out, and once the fans of the other bands left, the remains looked picked over. But we shrugged and took the stage. There was nothing left to do but put on the best show we could.

At this point we were fully formed. Steve, who went shirtless – exposing his hairy, puffed-out chest, wore a red cape and breeches. With ski goggles over his eyes and a green, plastic piggy bank strapped to his crotch, he'd thrust the protruding pig at the audience when he sang. He'd rattle loose change in the bank to the beat, which inspired the audience to scramble for coins to put in the slot. Gavin on the keyboard anchored the groove with funky Hammond-style keys and I took the front stage and banged a head-bouncing stomp with my congas and bongos. The girls sang back-up and shook tambourines and shekere rattles. Alex laid-down a funky guitar riff and the horn section blatted-out an accompanying shout.

Within seconds, we had the place grooving. We always got goofy stares when we set foot on stage, but when the music started; the heads nodded to each other and agreed "This is some cool shit." The woman who was with the passed out drunk, twisted in her seat, unable to avoid the funk -- eventually standing and shaking her hips. My friends Will and Tana had come to the show and were shocked at how the near-dead crowd came springing back to life. People heard us in the street and filtered in and danced like maniacs. Even the drunken snoozer had awoken and was dancing with his girlfriend like he was a *Soul Train* regular. By the time the girls took front stage and were singing *Tell Me Something Good*, we were burning the place down. People were going absolutely wild, knocking over tables and banging around like pinballs. A cluster of grizzled bikers, leftover from a country act, held chairs over their heads and did a Russian Barynya leg-kicking dance procession in a train before us. It was about as bonkers as 40 people could get at a show.

We played as good as we'd ever played that night and by the time we finished at midnight, the crowd roared in delight, having every ounce of sweat wrung from their bodies.

The fuse was officially lit. More than the spark that started our creative fire, the show was attended by Robert Elmes, the director of the Galapagos Art Space in Brooklyn, a premiere music venue in Williamsburg with a large back room that comfortably fit a few hundred people. With its man-made lake and bridge that greeted people upon entering, Galapagos was a unique music and art space. We took up a residency there and played a bi-monthly show to a growing fan base.

At first, we were the opening act for Gaijin a Go Go, a J-Pop band that was fronted by an Amazonian blond model named Petra Hanson. They were a mix of Asian and white musicians doing 60's style pop music... all tight-cut suits, go-go boots and swirling flower patterns. Paired with Night Wigga, we made for one of the most visually and musically unique bills in all of New York.

While Night Wigga gained popularity, we approached it with one foot in the legitimacy door and the other foot in an escapist fantasy for ourselves. At least, I did. I felt like I was on a ride to see where it took me. Almost like crowd surfing... the hands of the audience carrying me atop their fingers until my feet, or head hit the ground again. Steve and Gavin put time and energy into the band where as I simply showed up to perform, even though I was founding member. We played around New York City, partying like rock stars and rumbling drunkenly from one club to the next... riding a wave of craziness fueled by drugs and drink.

Then, 9/11 hit. Everything changed.

After the towers went down, the lower part of the city simmered with the scent of burnt flesh and dry wall. As close to war as I'll probably get, I suppose. Half of Manhattan was a DMZ. The streets below 14th street were car-less. There was plenty of time to walk the avenues and ponder how we got to that point... under the sunlit clouds of asbestos and lung fever.

And yet, under the terrible nature of that time... there was a beauty. The beauty of 9/12. The feeling of complete and total unity. There was an unspoken unity at that time... black, white, Hispanic, Asian... you could feel it. Just oneness among the city. And not just on the subways and sidewalks of Manhattan, but across the USA. If you saw a satellite photo of the tri-state area during the first few days after 9/11, it looked like a medical video of human veins as white blood cells attacked a virus. The country flooded New York to help.

The feeling lingered in New York for years. It felt so

good. There was mutual respect for everyone. It trickled down to everything.

Waiting in line people talked. They insisted you go first. Everything flipped. Old stuffy white women held doors open for young black men, which retuned a warm 'thank you,' which in turn broke into a deep conversation. This is just one example. You saw it everywhere... Conversations over coffee... pairing of people at tables you'd never seen before. New York City gelled in a way that it never had before.

On Halloween, I found myself with some friends at the infamous Winnie's Karaoke bar where Chinatown meets the Judiciary sector of lower Manhattan. After I belted out a decent rendition of Elvis Presley's *Love Me*, based solely on Nick Cage's version from the film *Wild At Heart*, I was crammed into a booth talking to an Asian girl named Fay in a green tinsel wig, and a black girl named Kriste in a blue tinsel wig. I exchanged numbers with them. A week later I invited them and others to have some drinks on my birthday at an Asian-fusion restaurant called Typhoon -- a converted Peruvian restaurant that looked like the Japanese redecorated Machu Picchu.

A few days later, I asked Kriste on a date and before I could say Shaka, she was my girlfriend, which thrilled my conservative white parents to pieces.

Kriste looked like Lauren Hill and sang Jazz standards with her smoky voice around Brooklyn and Manhattan with her piano playing partner, Tom. We were quite the striking pair Kriste and I. A six-foot tall, longhaired blond who resembled Sting's goofy brother and a five-foot-two Lauren Hill with a head full of squiggly Bantu knots.

Walking with her hand-in-hand in Union Square one day, an old black man stopped dead in his tracks and cocked his head like he saw a dinosaur. With all the disgust and betrayal of 400 years boiling inside of him, he mustered up a definitive "What, in the hell, are you doing with that honkey?" which stopped us dead in our tracks. We gave each other a kiss on the mouth and continued on our way.

Night Wigga thrived in that time. We continued to play as many shows as we could. Kriste was doubtful of our act. She saw us play and absorbed the crowd's visceral reaction, but she still felt like we were a bunch of fools phoning in some kind of minstrel show, which may or may not have been true.

Kriste was tough and a bit jaded from a life growing up where lines were definitely drawn. She was from North Carolina, living in Greenport, Brooklyn. She wasn't about to let shit like Night Wigga slide without her thoughts being known. Kriste's best friend was a tall black lesbian named Wendy. Wendy's girlfriend Charlie was a construction worker who walked on the high steel girders of Manhattan's skyscrapers. Good people... intellectuals all of them, but not exactly best friends with privileged white dudes who bounced around on stage in African costumes with their drunken buddies.

So, one random Tuesday night, the girls came to a Night Wigga show in Dumbo. They were amicable, open minded and drinking beer... but there was an air of put up or shut up and most of it was fueled by Kriste. Charlie and I couldn't have been more different, but eventually we found a common ground and warmed to each other over time.

For a Tuesday happy hour gig, the place was unusually crowded and some fans had come to show their support. We took the stage and kicked it into overdrive. We actually cranked up the kitsch factor and danced to the point of almost falling off the stage. But Wendy and Charlie got into the groove, and before long, they were partying and dancing with total conversion. Even Kriste saw how much fun we inspired and changed her tune a bit after that. Night Wigga was more than a cheap act... it was a group chock full of talented people that rounded into a very tight formation.

•••

We played all through the winter and as spring blossomed in, we got an invitation to a music festival in Woodstock New York, so we hopped in two cars and road-tripped it up there with only our costumes and equipment. During this trip, we went from being a group, to being a family... and with that, all the drama that goes with it.

The festival took place in a large barn that was converted into a bar and show space. We arrived around 6:00pm, just in time for cocktails, and blasted the place with our crazy energy. The sweet hippie, wallflower bartender had never seen anyone like us before. All of us wearing wild, African-styled garb, capes and sunglasses at night. By 9:00 we were on the stage and blowing the doors off the place. Most of the acts ranged from gentle singer-songwriters, coffeehouse country, light rock and some smatterings of grunge. But Night Wigga ramped up the party to 11. Steve shook the piggy bank, I banged the drums, we blared our horns and left everyone mesmerized.

Woodstock has a long history of music, festivals, radical artists and as a place to inspire and be inspired. But no one in those parts had ever seen anyone like us. We bombed the place like radicals and left everyone spinning like whirling dervishes. Our act wasn't just on stage... we spilled our crazy all over the place. We traveled in a large pack. A trip to the bar was an event. Ordering drinks in itself was a party. We'd grab a booth or a table in the corner and before you could blink, we'd have half the room in disco regalia. We'd sit on top of chairs, hang ornate banners, Light candles and smoke bushels of weed without care. People couldn't make heads or tails of us.

The party eventually moved to a bonfire outside and we all sat around drinking beer and smoking. I don't know where the beer came from. I don't know who was hosting or where we were to sleep. I think for Night Wigga, it was to be a two-day blast through... no sleep till Brooklyn. And that was exactly the case.

Both Abby and Christine took a liking to me, and I had to admit, I was finding it hard not to see them as well. They enjoyed wearing skimpy clothes, which rarely changed after shows and rehearsals. They could both dance extremely well, with seductive swinging hip moves that were hard to resist. Abby tried to make moves on me, but I knew Kriste was back in Brooklyn and I wanted to be faithful, so I skirted her advances.

At one point I slunk off to what I believed was either a caddyshack or some kind of groundskeeper's hang out and stuffed myself into a cold, faux leather sofa to try and get some rest. The birds were up with the white morning dawn and I got no sleep or rest whatsoever. I found my band mates all scratching their heads and asses and wondering where we might eat something. We had no hotel, no place to call home and no semblance of order. I'm not even sure there was a head person to guide us. We knocked on the doors of some mission café, but they were closed. An elder guy answered the door and apologized for having nothing to offer. Eventually, we went hungry.

Half our group hopped in Abby's White Honda and drove till we found what looked like a hostel and parked. We sat as the rain fell with the sunroof open. Steve knocked on the door, but no one answered. Abby and I got in a fight over the sunroof. She wanted it open and sprinkling on us... I wanted it closed. I got frustrated and left, which put me out in the rain regardless. I walked back to the show barn on foot, which took me about an hour.

The bar eventually opened and I ate a croissant and a coffee and when the rest of the band returned, they informed me the hostel opened and served them a massive breakfast.

We drank a few beers and by 11:00, we were on stage playing again to a strange amalgamation of hung-over bands and hippie locals. Somewhere along our trip, we lost my bongo stand, so instead of playing the bongos with my hands, I set my drums on chairs and smacked them with a wooden drumstick. It made a loud, hollow crack and my band mates countered by playing louder. We shook the gentle Sunday crowd's foundation to the core and left the stage with everyone stunned and probably -- a little relieved

The wallflower bartender had radically changed her look. The night before she was a longhaired hippie chick wearing a shapeless flower dress, but that Sunday morning, she'd gone full radical. Her hair was cut in a bob, with half her head buzzed down to the skull. She wore an orange and black motorcycle jacket, jeans and looked ready to ride off with a pack of wild animals. I couldn't help but think that Night Wigga had something to do with that. We infused our wild culture into every place we played and left them wanting more.

The festival committee shook our hands as we left and thanked us for not only making the trip, but for agitating the place in a way they've rarely seen.

•••

Back in NYC, Night Wigga was more popular than ever. Galapagos only fueled that fire and shows increased in size. We even had groupies, which seemed ridiculous as we still felt like a stumbling, bumbling work in progress and at times, no more than a novelty act.

Eventually, our one legitimate black member, Casey, left the band and we became a completely white group playing African music. But our fan base increased. Olga, a blond, borderline albino woman from Finland, followed us religiously. She started a fan club and not only was she in Woodstock with us, she appeared at every show without fail.

The peak of our powers arrived in the middle of the April. Night Wigga was invited to perform at the birthday party of Felicia Collins, the guitarist of The Most Dangerous Band In the World, led by Paul Schafer on Late Night With David Letterman. She caught us at a random show and loved us.

Her birthday was going to be a showcase of acts that would play for her and she was to close her own birthday show as the final act.

The place, a chic venue on the edge of Soho and Chinatown, was rocking and there were legitimate players at the show... fashion models, musicians, and influential people wearing more money on their wrists than I had in the bank.

A week before, Felicia saw us play at a show in midtown that was a complete shit-show of a performance. We sounded bad, played without passion and Steve even asked the audience at one point "How do we sound?" with a positive response from the crowd. But Steve turned to us on the stage and said half-heartedly "Well it sounds like shit up here." And he was right... mainly because of the sound system, which made it hard to hear the set, but we were half-assing it with no form or spirit. So at Felicia Collins' birthday bash, we felt compelled to turn up the Night Wigga charm. Ramp up the crazy and blow the doors off the place.

We had a full group. 12 of us in all. 4 horns, 3 percussionists, Steve and the girls, Alex and Gavin and a head full of alcohol and weed to power us through. We were the opening act and in charge of setting the tone. The tension was palpable as the sound system cut the house music, leaving us to fill the quiet with our groove. I'm not sure why but Steve started the drum machine and walked away -- just went into the shadows and left me up front in the spotlight alone. *Layla*. Probably our tightest song and also our most popular. We never made a set list and Steve dictated the song choices randomly.

I had my full set of drums on stands in front of me,

but I was banging a single tom drum that was slung around my shoulder at my side on a sling. I grabbed the beat and just crept up to the mic and layed down a sweet bop. Heads began to turn. I rapped the drum rapidly and got a few whooos from the bar. Even Felicia, who swung around on her stool to face us, smiled widely. I swung the tom around my back and started attacking my congas and bongos like I'd been doing it my whole life. The place came alive.

Then, the girls stepped up and danced in Unison. Perfectly, like they'd done it a million times. I had the stage for a solid minute before Steve, shirtless, holding his cape above his head like Dracula, emerged from the shadows and grabbed the mike. He thrust his hips forward and shook the piggy bank coins in perfect unison to the beat, holding the mic to his crotch. The crowd clapped and cheered. The girls rocked their tambourines and Shekras and the rest of the band kicked it with us. The place went fucking wild. Every head turned and people just spilled onto the dance floor. Felicia grinned so wide, I could see it almost hurt her face. She put her hands in the air and waved them like she just didn't care.

Steve sang in his deep timber "What do you do when you get lonely...hey hey hey" and the place got crazy loose. During Layla, the girls would do a unison-backing shout where they'd sing, "Fuck me, fuck me, fuck me got to have me sugar!" We totally and completely set the place on fire. We were to do three songs and only 20 minutes, but after our second song, *Magic Man*, we'd chewed up the time. An encore kept us there another 10 minutes and closed the set with *Tell Me Something Good*, which kept the place bouncing until the next act came on stage.

Felicia thanked us for a great opening set as we took over the huge corner booth that fit all of us comfortably. We smoked enough weed to kill a horse and drank tequila all night. The rest of the party thought we were a riot. We turned the booth into a circus tent and bounced around like clowns, entertaining the crowd long after we left the stage.

A few days later, the New York Press wrote in their music review that "Night Wigga is either the best band in New York City, or the worst."

High praise for sure... I suppose.

•••

The summer was a blur. New York went into a spin cycle wash of love and much of the pain of 9/11 was alleviated with drinking, smoking and partying. The spirit of New York hadn't been higher. It took a tragedy to make that happen. But the town was on a continuous self-medicated ride as it both healed and broke simultaneously.

In the middle of the sweltering heat, my buddy Will was getting married in South Carolina. I was one of his groomsmen, so Kriste and I rented a car and drove there in one 17-hour stretch.

This may come as a shock, but people in South Carolina can be a little uncomfortable around mixed-race couples. I wore a tux to the wedding and Kriste tried to discreetly blend into the background by wearing a short, fire engine red dress that hugged every ounce of her curvaceous little body. When she and I first met, I had longer hair, but now it was short and spiked -- bleach-blonde from the sun. We were quite the pair. Will's friends thought I was the most eccentric person they'd ever met. A tall white guy with his black girlfriend. During the reception where the entire town showed up for free food and dancing, Kriste sat on my knee and a group of about 12 people surrounded us like celebrities. They wondered what I thought of this po-dunk town and how bored I must have been. Little did they know it was just perfect... a sweet little town with one blinking stoplight and all the country cookin' you could eat. I was on vacation and yes, New York City was all it was cracked up to be and more, but I may have been cracking up a bit and South Carolina was as good a place as any to spackle the cracks shut with gravy, biscuits and fried pickle slices.

Kristie even made fun of me later in the hotel room -- mocking me about how the boys had surrounded me... asked me questions like I was some exotic man with some fascinating black girlfriend in a red dress. And to them, maybe I was. But I was just a guy, trying to figure it all out just like them. I just happened to be in South Carolina for a wedding.

As the summer of 2002 ended and Fall blew in, Kriste and I started to unravel. We were different people, and none of that had to do with our looks or background.

She was conservative, I was wild.

She was grounded, I was structureless.

She was an intellectual and I was a smart ass.

She wanted uniformity and I was living in complete chaos. On a warm autumn weekend, Kriste went to Chicago with Tom to do a few shows at a Jazz festival. I did a lifeless

Saturday night gig in midtown with the band. Afterwards, I found myself in bed with Olga, which spilled into Sunday. She and I hung out and watched football on my tiny 18-inch tube TV and got to know each other. She was a drifter and Night Wigga was just another band she latched onto for the ride.

That night, after Olga left, Kriste rolled into town. We'd planned to meet in Brooklyn at her place, but she wanted to crash at mine after the bus ejected her and Tom at the Port Authority bus terminal on 42nd street. She was beat and headed almost immediately for bed. She was met with Olga's necklace and earrings -- sprawled on the nightstand like they were on display at Macy's. She knew right away what it meant. I made some sort of excuse that the band was there and everyone passed out in the place and that I actually slept on the floor, but she saw right through it. She actually slept in the bed, which I knew was hard for her because it was desecrated. We clung to each other a few more weeks, but broke apart soon after.

I turned my attention to the band. At this point, we were in full-on crazy mode. Not only did we play together, we hung together and dated each other. The perpetual party never seemed to stop. Christine and I got close and eventually hooked up. This made Abby, who still had a huge crush on me, really angry. Not only did it cause her to turn a cold shoulder to me, she stopped speaking to me. I don't think she understood why I chose Christine over her and she was probably right. Abby was smart, cute and incredibly sexy, but I just fell into whatever gravitational pull I got caught up in...

which happened to be Christine. Abby started dating Steve and now we had two couples in the band. The band dynamics got nuttier. We were like Fleetwood Mac, only less talented.

Then something subtle happened that changed the band. It was a small, yet cutting incident that for me, changed the tone of the environment.

During a practice at Steve's, we all got intensely stoned on some high-grade weed. Our trumpet player, a sweet cherub-like guy named Brian was in the kitchen with our guitar player Alex, a big, burly guy with long brown hair usually pulled into a ponytail. Alex tended to be a bit grouchy. We could hear them talking but it turned cold. Brian lost his boundaries and got too close to Alex, who told him numerous times to "back off."

Then a loud smack!

Alex popped Brian across the face with an open-palmed smack. Brian stumbled into the living room with a look of hurt and dejection -- his eyes welling with tears.

We immediately got to the bottom and Alex explained what happened – personal space was broken, etc. But the damage was done. A few apologies passed back and forth, but the hurt in Brian's eyes really sunk into me.

Bands fight and argue, but this was ugly. Night Wigga seemed to hit the backend of the summit and were sliding down the other side.

Brian left the band soon after.

•••

On a cold night, after another lifeless gig in Williamsburg in front of almost no one in a strange industrial bar under
the Williamsburg Bridge, we all parted ways into the night.
Steve and Abby were catching a cab to Borough Hall and
Christine and I were going to walk to the L Train and ride
back to the East Village where we both lived.

As we walked – the wind kicking off the water and
cutting us to the bone – we noticed a running car parked on
the side of the road. As we passed and cocked our heads back,
we saw that no one was inside. A small grey Honda or Toyota,
just puttering… tailpipe coughing out little puffs of smoke…
without a driver.

Christine and I looked at each other.

She said, "Get in!" and I scooted to the passenger
side. She hopped behind the wheel and within seconds, we
were tooling down the street. We couldn't believe it.

"What the hell are we doing?" I shouted.

"Getting a free ride." Christine said, maniacally navigating the wheel into the buzzing night traffic.

Within seconds we were driving over the Williamsburg Bridge. Suddenly we were on Delancey, made a right on
Essex, which turned into Avenue A, and we pulled over and
parked next to Tompkins Square park at 9th Street.

Couldn't have taken more than five minutes.

We cut the engine, got out and left the car for the cops
to find later. We snuck around the corner and hit a nameless
dive bar on Avenue B and 10th street. Even though we were
drunk from our gig and high from the adrenaline rush of thiev-
ery, we drank hard and stumbled from the place at midnight.

I felt tired and wanted to go home. I leaned towards

my apartment on 9th street. She tugged my arms and yanked me towards her place on Avenue C.

She said "Make love to me" and I said no, which is a window into my soul at the time. She yanked me again and moaned, "Please. Come make a baby with me."

Alarm bells rang in my head. That was as a good a time to NOPE out of there as any time I could remember in my life.

Christine was fun and a good time, but I was not about to settle down with her... or anyone at the time. I was feeling heavy... tired in my bones.

I pulled my arm away and told her I needed to get some rest. I swooped in for a disorienting hug, squeezed her tight, released her, spun her around and shoved her off like a child towards the depths of Alphabet city. She stumbled away and managed a dejected, drunken wave goodbye.

Winter hit and so did the new year of 2003. I became friendly with a cute Columbian girl named Catalina who worked the soup station at a small café named Medina around the corner from my office on 17th Street. I asked her out and we started dating. Catalina was petite, with dark curly hair and big brown eyes. She was a bookworm and quiet. Maybe exactly what I needed.

Although Kriste and I didn't work out, Catalina was stabilizing, mellow and rarely said much. She got caught up in the whirlwind of my life and spun along with me. She came to some Night Wigga shows, but the sonic thunder would steamroll her against the wall, making her more of a wallflower than she already was.

Christine felt alienated, but we weren't exactly an "official" couple, so nothing was said but the feelings got funky. Abby didn't talk to me anymore, but she made it clear Catalina wasn't welcomed either. Some nights we played without our horn section, which forced others to overplay, or reinvent our songs with a stripped-down sound. Sometimes it worked, sometimes it was just painful.

One night Gavin and I were the only members to show for a snowy gig at a dive Irish bar in a dirty back room in Brooklyn, so we melded with another group who also lost half their act. Gavin played keys, I played the bongos, and the two guys from a band named Sugar Snacks played guitar and sang. We came on as Night Sugar and did some covers. We did a slow, grinding, almost erotic 7-minute version of *Like a Virgin*, which transfixed the slumming white-collar crowd into a state of piqued interest.

After the show, the singer said "we should start a band" and I looked at Gavin who chuckled and shrugged. We were already in a band, and at that moment, I wasn't sure I wanted to be in one anymore.

•••

Spring came and the Night Wigga train was coming into a station. Where that station was, I didn't know. After two years together we decided to make a demo album. We recorded it at Gavin's apartment in Park Slope, Brooklyn. We spent a day clumsily banging through our three classics… Layla, Magic Man and Life In The Vaseline (Life in the fast Lane). It was as unprepared and wayward as we'd always played. Perhaps that was where our magic lied. Perhaps that's how I approached it… one foot in… one foot out. Gavin and Steve edited the recordings into a semblance of our sound, although no horns appeared on the tracks other than electric wails Gavin supplied through his keyboards. My drums were essentially missing from the recordings and at that point, I didn't care. I wasn't even Ringo in this version of the band's recording, I was percussion guy #2 in the background.

I sat in my apartment and listened to the final songs we burned on CD. There I was nearing the end…. at the beginning again, listening to Steve's growl like I did two years prior when he sent me the MP3 of him singing Bill Wither's *Use Me*.

The first time, the idea of a band was electric and mysterious… even fun. After a two-year party… grinding it out on every darkened stage in Brooklyn and blasting our ferocious sense of belligerent crazy at festivals and showcases… the magic seemed to have disappeared.

The last show we did together as a complete line-up act was another showcase. It took place at BAM, one of Brooklyn Museum of Arts smaller, more experimental spaces whose name escapes me. It was a series of multiple acts, playing music in multiple rooms simultaneously. Projectors flashed images and lights against the wall with performing bands. Patrons wandered in and out of each space at their leisure. Some spaces had walls that glowed, some rooms had films projecting. Some of us wandered into other rooms and saw bands play, then we'd wander back and played ourselves.

Catalina was there and she was pressed against the wall like she entered an insane asylum. It was pure madness and not fun at all. In fact, it drove me to near insanity. We weren't playing music anymore, we'd become an art piece, a puzzle piece that fit into a strange narrative and I didn't understand it.

I watched Catalina, her face contorted in a smile and almost in pain... having to deal with the art installation she was trapped in. Her face changed colors... over and over... purple, white, green, pink. It felt like one big stupid slide show or some kind of bad experimental trip and we were all stuck and unable to escape. Again, we were all super high and drunk and the flashing lights and unanchored feeling of disoriented madness made me psychotic.

My memory is hazy. We performed at this show and I remember leaving the room and entering another room and seeing Gaijin a Go Go.

Gaijin a Go Go, the band we'd been linked to for a while was signed by Sony Music and had released their first album. Again, we were on the opening bill. I actually did some art and graphics for invitations and promotions for them and for us. But I don't remember the show. This wasn't their album release party... but it was a showcase for them of some kind... I can't remember anymore.

My brain was scrambled eggs at this point. Between working all day, playing all night, heavy drinking and smoking, and dragging my drums through the streets of Manhattan and Brooklyn, I was pretty much finished. And not with Night Wigga... music in general.

I was over-tired and under nourished... over-sexed and under duress. The band became a job to me and when that happens, the party is over.

In the middle of Spring 2003, I went to Steve's apartment for another night of practice. Yet this time I came clean... unencumbered by drums or equipment. I hadn't brought any beer and dressed in clothes more in tune to work in an office than to sweat through while banging on bongos.

Everyone sensed it when I came in. I was all business. I sat on a footstool in the middle of the room and clasped my hands together. I was a head lower than everyone. Not in a position of power.

"What's going oooon?" Steve warbled with a hint of humor and nerves.

I told them I was out... that I wasn't into the band anymore and it was time to leave. Abby made it clear I wasn't welcome anyway. I don't recall everyone's reaction, but my news was met with the general thought that I was "a quitter."

But that's how it can be with bands. We were a family -- a dysfunctional family, but still a family. We spent two years crushing New York together, through the ups and downs... through some of the most extreme highs I've had, to some pretty low lows. So leaving felt like a foundation piece cracked off and brought instability to everyone.

I left the apartment with a general sense of anger from the group. Disappointment. I believe I was even told to "leave" if that's how I felt about things. If I was to leave, they were going to shame me about it, and it somehow made my decision even easier in the moment, but it stung as I hit the streets.

I wandered aimlessly in Brooklyn and even got lost. I

asked people on the street where a 4 train might be and people didn't know. I wasn't even sure I was in Brooklyn anymore.

Eventually, I found the Brooklyn Bridge and walked across. It was cold and I wasn't dressed warm enough. But it felt like a cleansing. A ritual of cold pain to excise the demons I'd created for myself. But in reality, I felt an unbelievable sense of relief.

I wasn't a good musician... or a musician at all, if I was being honest with myself. So leaving the band was like releasing myself from a self-made prison where I could breathe again. I stepped off the Night Wigga train just as easily as I stepped on it.

A few weeks later, I sold my entire drum set on Craigslist. Bongos, Congas... stands... everything. I sold them cheap.

When the buyer came to get them, a slim Hispanic guy with a fetching moustache, he slapped the money in my palm and he and his friend snagged the stuff like a smash-and-grab robbery. Perhaps they thought I'd change my mind about the price. They didn't talk, make eye contact or say goodbye. Just grabbed the gear and split as my spring-loaded door closed in my face.

Took about 10 seconds.

That was 20 years ago. I haven't played the drums again since.

About a month later, Steve called me on the phone. My landline. I was literally about to take it off the wall and go completely cellular when it rang and I answered.

Steve and I talked sweetly to each other. About the

start... the finish... the great years in-between. After that call we never spoke again.

I never spoke to Christine, Gavin, Olga or anyone from the band again. Never even *saw* them. It was a clean break.

Catalina and I continued on together and another chapter of my life closed like one of Catalina's many books. It wasn't intentional. There was no animosity on my end. I just caught another set of crazy waves that carried me along like the many I'd surfed my entire life.

•••

One lazy summer day, around 2017, when my son was about seven, I was flipping through my vast iTunes collection of music and DJ-ing random songs to my family while they sat on the couch.

Like most children, my son was discovering music and he wanted to hear what I had to offer. I introduced him to as many songs as a seven-year-old might find accessible. Beach Boys, The Beatles and Steely Dan. I eventually let the shuffle give us random choices and of course, the wheel of fortune gave us Night Wigga. *Layla*, to be precise.

Max's ears pricked up, and his head rose like a flower to the sun.

"What's this?" he asked vibrantly.

All the other selections passed over him like background noise. Nothing caught his interest at all. Nothing catchy from Rubber Soul... nothing sweet from Endless Summer... not even the effervescent voices of ABBA could pique his interest. But somehow, the first 20 seconds of Night Wigga's *Layla* yanked his ear and temporarily stole his attention from the drawing pad.

"Oh this?" I said nonchalantly, "just a weird band from New York City."

He bobbed his head and continued to scratch images into his drawing pad with a long #2 pencil.

"You like it?" I asked innocently.

"Yea." he said smiling. "I like it."

THE DEATH OF OUR DREAMS

TEETH, TATTOOS
AND TOES

The other day I saw a guy smile and my eyes went right to his teeth. They were unnaturally white. Absurdly white. His smile could have been seen from the international space station.

We live in a world where everyone is super clean and buzzed tight. Back in the 70's, hair was everywhere and 90% of the population looked as though they'd smoked nine packs of unfiltered Marlboro cigarettes since the day they were born. Have you ever seen a porno from the late seventies? The actors had so much hair between their legs, it looked as if they had a Boston fern in a leg lock. Many times, you couldn't see what member was entering which hole.

Now hair is preened to a fine finish, teeth sparkle like diamonds and pubic hair is zipped into fine strips. Is this an improvement on the way we look and feel? I believe so. Sure, some natural style goes a long way. Some men would look better if they avoided the buzz cut look, and some women could do without extreme hair highlights. But for the most part, we're cleaner and more styled and all the better for it.

A lot of countries think Americans wash too much—which is probably true. We think if you don't smell like a freshly picked flower in a vase of cologne, you're borderline offensive. Some countries go a pretty long time without showering and they consider the smell of a natural body alluring. Pheromones are released through sweat glands and pores, so if they're clogged with fragrant lotions and washes, we might stop the natural breeding process. Considering how overcrowded the planet is, perhaps not. I think skipping a day to let the natural oils build back onto the skin and hair is important.

But the "pearly whites" …they're not so pearly as much as flashlight white these days. You shouldn't look as though you clicked in a set of Dracula fangs from the Halloween store. They should look… well, pearly and natural. We have access to professional grade whitening products for home use and they're a fraction of the expensive treatments, but people abuse them like crack cocaine. Yellow teeth are gross, but teeth that look like you rolled a coat of Benjamin Moore Ultra Bright White over them is just wrong.

My wife is a dedicated brusher. Her teeth are clean and white. She brushes four times a day and often looks like a rabid dog. She had bad teeth growing up and was forced to get some of them replaced in a few spots. Now her smile is razor sharp.

Speaking of razor sharp, my son recently got braces. I thought they'd be more streamlined than the chain-link fence

I had in my face as a kid, but apparently, they're still just as bad. After the doctor finished hammering in the railroad spikes into his mouth, he evacuated the crew so the 5:15 could arrive on time.

Unfortunately, my teeth aren't so great even though I had braces. My fangs were butchered by my orthodontist/ sadomasochist, Dr. Schneider. He thought it was a good idea to grind a few of them to nubs with a buzz saw. He jammed a disk-sander into my mouth and pressed down with all his weight until they left a trail of smoke that summoned a crew of forest fire rangers. But I've done a decent job of maintaining them with continuous brushing and flossing.

I've also used whitening strips to erase years of smoking and coffee drinking I lacquered over them. But I stopped once they were at a natural looking white. Some people keep whitening to the point of looking fake. Having natural teeth that look fake is pointless, but like a lot of things, some people just can't stop. Like eating Cheetos. You can't eat just one…

I think that's an ad campaign.

Toothpastes have whitening formulas built in them so you get a treatment when you brush. There's also whitening mouthwashes, pre-brushing treatments and whitening chewing gum as well. At this rate, the color yellow may be eliminated from our color spectrum.

There's so many toothpastes now I don't know which one to get. There's regular paste, gel, a paste and gel twist, tartar control, whitening, tartar with whitening, tartar with whitening and mouthwash, tartar whitening… you get the point. There's so many combinations you need to borrow a NASA rocket scientist to figure it out. They have names like Control and Total and Complete. I'm convinced I need the best so the toothpaste can destroy germs and particles. But the fancier the toothpaste, the more expensive it gets. You pick up a pack of extra cool mint gel tartar control whitening paste with peroxide, baking soda and Listerine Complete and it tastes like you gargled with a chemistry set. The box has sparkling graphics from the future that lures you into a purchase.

The home whitening kits are pouring off the shelves. There's trays you squeeze goo into and slide over your grill like a sports mouth guard. Paints you brush on and zap with a frightening blue light. Swabs you massage into the enamel and let sit. Electric brushes that jackhammer whiteness into the teeth. They have names like Optical, Crystal, Bright, Glow, Luminescent and other labels that make you shield your eyes.

But what are all these products doing to our teeth? Is the long-term effect damaging? So many things erode the enamel on our teeth as it is. I once had someone scream at me for sucking on a lemon because it "ERODES THE ENAMEL!" For the love of Pete, if a lemon is damaging to teeth, I can only imagine what a strip of whitening chemicals is doing to the ol' chompers.

But I guess many people don't think about the long haul. They'll bake in the sun, smoke cigarettes and whiten their teeth till they look like a 1984 Coppertone magazine ad and pay the price later.

When you look as perfect as a mannequin, you attract other mannequin-like people and when you're natural looking, you attract natural looking people. But what is natural? Have we gotten so far away from what natural looks like that we can't go back? Natural people from way back when didn't pump iron and have rock-hard chiseled abs. They didn't do isolation workouts for the core and make the glutes look so round you could bounce a quarter off them, they looked... natural.

There's a balance we need to have in our modern day. The sun is good in small batches, fatty foods good in small amounts and the whiteness of our teeth the shade of a newly popped oyster pearl.

I personally could never be on High-Definition TV because I have face pores that you could drive a Mack truck through. I try and keep my face clean, pores clear and my teeth clean, but I don't overdo it. The world is changing and TV talent will be based on a new set of criteria besides personality and the ability to speak well. It will also require China-doll skin and teeth that gleam like the sun.

These people are not real in many ways. They exist in a vacuum of perpetual pampering and dermatologist visits. They have really big lollypop heads and teeth the size of highway billboards. On TV they seem fine, but see them in real life and you're shocked by how short, tan, clean, slicked (fill in any reaction here) they are.

So, lay off the whitening strips if you can. Yes, coffee and smoking can make the teeth look crusty. Years of food and drink can dull the shine. But clean up the clackers for a natural look. If you're turning heads because your teeth look like reflectors that a jogger puts on their clothing for a night run, time to chuck the white strips in the trash and switch to regular old bubble gum.

•••

There's a philosophy about tattoos that I adhere to and that's "go big the first time." If you go small, you could face a lifetime of random art choices that pop up over your body like subway graffiti. By the time it's all said and done, you could resemble the bedroom wall that was scribbled on by a three-year-old. If you get addicted to tattoos, every patch of clear flesh will eventually get coated in color. That's when people get desperate for personal real estate and tattoo the whites of their eyes, their tongues or their liver.

This is coming from someone with no tattoos, so perhaps I shouldn't talk. But I do love tattoos. I once put a down payment on a tattoo that I planned to etch across my back -- a giant Chinese dragon with flames and water done in a sepia tone to match my natural blonde coloring. But when I found out I was having a kid, that money went to diapers. It's probably just as well. They say once you get one tattoo, you get more and that's how the whole scribble thing starts. But tattoos can be expensive and you can use that money for baby food or to have tattoos removed.

Being an artist, I've drawn tattoos for people and they're literally walking around with my art on their bodies. I've also drawn tattoos for myself that I never pulled the trigger on. If I had, I would probably be regretful because I've had some pretty bad ideas for tattoos. I was going to tattoo a big scorpion on the back of my neck and now that I'm 50, I'm happy I didn't. Scorpions are cool, but tattoos can also be a daily reminder of the dumb shit you were into at certain points of your life and that's what scrapbooks are for. Looking in the mirror can be a constant reminder of your past hobbies. There's no way to avoid mirrors because we need to comb our hair and brush our teeth and we do these things shirtless at times.

Tattoos can be a roadmap of your life… your trauma, your pain, your crazy adventures… but Bart Simpson pissing on your ankle, or a SpongeBob Square Pants coming out of your ass crack can have people questioning your sanity and your ability to make quality choices.

I used to buy tattoo magazines and some of the tattoos were both amazing and stupefying. People were canvases… living masterpieces, but some people seemed to hate themselves. It was a strange dichotomy. Severed bloody heads on your thigh are cool when you're 25, but at 85 they terrify the staff of the nursing home you're rotting away in.

Prominently featured in these magazines was a person named ManWoman, who was covered in swastikas. His ultimate goal was to snatch the Nazi connotation of it and return it back to a place where it was featured prominently among the Greeks and Native Americans. But people see swastikas and think Nazis. As someone who works in advertising and marketing -- an industry where you constantly have to educate the client and customer, it must be exhausting telling everyone you meet that your swastikas are the *friendly* kind and more spiritual. Unfortunately, Hitler stomped all over that ideal, so your life may be dedicated to telling every person you see that your swastikas are the happy kind.

People seem to love getting Chinese symbols tattooed down their spine and across their arms even though they're not Chinese and know nothing about Chinese culture. Chinese symbols are beautiful and stylish, but many unknowingly have a menu tattooed across their chest or a recipe for General Tso's Chicken stamped on their lower back. They display it proudly and friends inexplicably get hungry.

Tattoos can speak volumes that words could never express. They can tell people who you are... or were. The holy cross, the faces of your children or robot parts will tell someone about your dedication to god, family or what correctional facility you were recently released from. Tattoos can be administered by professionals or your prison bunkmate who pressed a heated ballpoint pen into your back. They say a tear tattoo on your cheek represents the number of people you've killed in prison. I'm not sure if it's true, but when I see people with tear tattoos on their cheek, I treat them with kindness because not only are they cold, vicious killers, but they appear sad, and I like to make sad people feel better when I can.

Tattoos are your personality. They let the viewer know "Hey, I'm totally insane. Are you insane as well?"

Or they can say, 'are you a fan of Iron Maiden like me?' Do you like H.R. Giger, The Hobbit, octopuses, majestic suns, The Indian god Ganesha, eyeballs, dragons (both Asian and fantasy), Boba Fett, wolves in the moonlight, lotus flowers, swords slicing through roses, sailors, anchors, hula girls with ukuleles, clawing lions, yin and yang, tropical fish, day of the dead girls, snakes, skulls or tribal birds? ...Me too!

That kind of identification is useless if you entered a tattoo shop and got something off the flash board. A skull with a top hat or a chubby blue jay with a ribbon are common. The black panther crawling up a leg or an eagle with an American flag are yawn inducing. You'd like to think a tattoo expresses your life and mentality. Tattoos are permanent and should be thought about. Telling someone to "give me whatever you want" should be reserved for bartenders and not someone with an ink gun buzzing permanent images into your flesh. Over the past decade, the tattoo has been creeping up the torso to be featured prominently on the neck. Neck tattoos can be sexy, but that sex appeal is usually reserved for plump-assed hip hop artists whose teeth have more gold than the average person's bank account. Or rock stars whose job it is to drip sweat on stage and a shirt is optional most of the time. A complicated tattoo across the neck of the girl manning KFC's chicken fryer? The sex appeal disappears. I'm not frowning on people with jobs, and people should get tattoos wherever they want, but maybe get out of your teens and your minimum wage job before you have an image the size of your hand stenciled across your throat.

Many tattoo shops won't tattoo people who are drunk or on drugs and that's a good policy. Folks love to fall into tattoo shops late at night and demand a full sized tattoo of Bill Murray across their entire body. These are responsible tattoo artists. But there's also tattoo artists who can't spell and have yet to know the difference between They're, Their and There. There's a lot of NO REGERTS, BLOOD IS THICKER THEN WATER, and LIVE YOU'RE BEST LIFE walking the streets of the world.

Tattoos represent ancient culture. They can bring us back to primitive times. The New Zealand Maori tattoo their faces and many African cultures practice scarification. This gets interpreted in modern times as barbed wire and swirling firebirds. The only culture the modern city dweller has is the hard concrete of an office building and the general disdain of

9 to 5 culture so they get back to the tribal by wrapping their bodies in geometric banding and gaping their earlobes enough to toss a cornhole bag through.

These are personal choices, guided by the voices of their ancestors and heavy bong hits. If chanting around giant bonfires on 5th avenue weren't frowned upon, they'd do it. We chant and stomp and become primitive because it's the best reaction to the growing stiffness of the grinding corporate sterilization. We reach into our souls and wear our insides on the outsides. Our skin become hieroglyphics and we literally wear hearts on our sleeves. We quietly shift through life, hiding under pictures while they speak for us like storybooks.

The tattoo is now more prominent on the face. They say the eyes are the window to the soul, but what about another set of eyes below those eyes? There's a guy who tattooed an entire skull across his face. That's a grim creative choice. I'm not sure if he has a romantic partner and I'm not sure he cares. At some point you may want a companion and while skulls are cool, kissing them romantically is another matter. Hey, whatever floats your boat.

A lot of NBA players have tattoos. As far as pro athletes go, basketball players show the most skin, with their arms being exposed completely. There's a lot of bad tattoos in pro sports. Mainly because these guys have looked 25 since they were 12 and simply walked into a shop and got tagged without needing ID. If you think people make bad creative choices at 19, what do you think a 14-year-old will have done?

The worst tattoo you can get is someone's name. Especially if they are not your child. Get a name tattooed on your bicep; the universe will break you apart before the scab heals. There's a famous Normal Rockwell painting of a sailor getting a woman's name tattooed on his arm with a list of others that have been crossed out. This is not a total fabrication. This happens all the time. Jonny Depp famously got *Winona Forever* tattooed on his arm and that was a sure-fire guarantee that the relationship would end. He had it changed to *Wino Forever*. If he sobers up, he'll have to change that too.

Now tattoo artists do a lot of cover-ups. The unicorn dancing on a rainbow you got in 1983 needs a makeover and a tattoo guy is happy to plaster a black crow over it. Some of these cover-ups are incredibly well done. They take elements of the old tattoo and weave it into the new tattoo.

Of course, if you want the tattoo gone forever, there's the laser. Technology has finally caught up with us. Back in 1955, we thought we'd be piloting flying cars on our way to our space station pods. Lasers would be used for everything from cooking a turkey dinner to slicing metal blocks like warm butter. Instead we use them to correct our vision and blast tattoos off our flesh. The modern eraser. Instead of a horrible creative choice you made at 19, you'll have a horrible blotch of scar tissue instead. One is preferable to the other. Now the warning of "Are you sure? This is permanent!" is replaced with "ahhh, if you don't like it, you can get it lasered off." Tattoos can be expensive, but you know what's really expensive? Laser tattoo removal!

You can get a tattoo flush with cash and a few years later; you're broke and looking for money to have it removed. You can apply for a job, but the hiring manager is having problems looking into your eyes because you have a bunch of eyes tattooed on your face.

•••

Nails are a big deal. The painting, the trimming the coloring. My wife sits down with a tray of equipment and you'd think she was going into major surgery... removing someone's gal bladder or a brain. But she's just doing her nails.

She has scrapers, scoopers, cutter and sanders. The sanders are big, small, long and short. They're metal and paper. Colored and plain. It takes a fine wood-worker to understand all the sanding paper weights. There's pinchers and grabbers, scalpels and cutters. Things that look like hoes and garden tools.

Women go through a long and arduous routine to get their toenails into a state of beautification. A man's routine is to cover his crumpled, hairy claw with a thick sock in hopes that when it's uncovered a few days later, the sweat and friction has miraculously rubbed the layers of dead skin off and bled the yellow out of his overgrown talons.

Nail painting is much like house painting. I should know, I painted houses for eight years. There's the paint removal, which involves chemicals that can curl wallpaper. Cotton balls that litter the place like bunnies. Then the scraping, sanding and the hammering. Then the surgical equipment comes in. The sculpting and cutting. Removing dead skin... removing living skin! The shaping and prep work is enormous. Much like the house painter, more work goes into the pre-prep. The spackle and sanding is the hard part... the painting is easy.

The amount of nail polish colors at the store rival any

Benjamin Moore chip rack. There's so many shades of red, you need an electron microscope to know the difference. My wife tests a few colors of red and asks me which one I like better. They all look the same, but at this point I know better to say anything, so I point at a finger and say the "middle finger, definitely!" Sometimes that's the right choice; sometimes it leads to a discussion about why I chose that color. I need to justify the decision and then we get into feelings and how colors evoke reactions and emotions.

My wife asks me what color pairs with her red Christmas outfit. There's no correct answer. I usually ask which one SHE likes, and work off of that. But then she says "I'm asking you" and I get nervous. I try and pair a red wine with the decision and before I know it, we're down a slippery path. My decision is met with a lot of "Are you sures?" and by day two, I'm firm on my decision. "Most definitely" I say with the utmost confidence. In fact it gets to the point where I start to champion the nail color decision. I start using words like *fabulous* and *breathtaking* and her decision to use French tips is set as solid as concrete foundation.

Then we get to the toes. Sometimes the colors on the toenails will match with the fingernails, sometimes they don't. Apparently, I'm supposed to know when. Like when I shouldn't wear white anymore because it's a certain time of the year. The difference between the finger and toenails is as different as North and South America.

The toes get soaked in water and they get a similar, yet different routine. The toenails get a clipper that looks like hedge clippers and are chopped at the tops and again, sanded with boards.

My wife has a funky toe that needs special attention. The nail on her left big toe had a fungus that stunted its growth. It looks like the toe of a cartoon character after it was whacked by a wooden mallet. It's my job to take care of this dwarf beast. I attack the thing with a mini spin-sander. I wear a mask and eye protection so I don't get the fugusy dust into my lungs. If I answered the door, you'd think I was belt sanding the staircase railing. But it's just one tiny toenail. The nail is thicker than a deer skull and a shade of color that you won't find on the nail polish rack.

Once I've sanded a few layers off the nail, I coat it with a medicine lacquer which I believe does nothing because when I return to do it again a few weeks later, it looks the exact same. Her dermatologist told us it would require a lot of dedication and passion to get this nail right and I felt like we needed to renew our wedding vows before tackling this nail. I held Rita's hand and together we left his office with a determination and grit usually reserved for someone about to step out of a flying airplane.

My wife loves to do her nails. It takes her hours and they come out great. Unfortunately, once they're done, she's unable to do much of anything around the house. Either they're in a state of drying, or in a state of potentially getting chipped. And we can't have that! Suddenly my responsibilities triple. I went from simply eating dinner -- to cooking dinner, eating dinner and cleaning up after dinner. I ask Rita for something and she's like "Nope sorry, can't do it" while her fingers are pointed in the air like a surgeon waiting for the assistant to yank rubber gloves over her hands. She's leaning back in a chair, blowing air on them regardless of how long it's been. I could return home hours later, and she could have been playing Beethoven's 5th symphony on a piano for all I know. But once I enter the kitchen, the fingers are up in the air and she's shaking them like they're on fire... "Just did a third coat" she reveals.

Many women have their nails done in a nail spa. Many men as well. I did it once and it felt great. Some places massage your feet and pamper your fingers and toes like tiny babies. They call it a nail spa, but it's hard to truly relax in a place where the workers are in a state of abject misery. I've never seen a nail spa worker look happy to grind the boils off some well-heeled lady's hammertoe.

Let's face it; unless you've got a fetish, the feet are people's least favorite part of the body. They're easily the most neglected. Kind of like car tires. You don't pay much attention to them unless they're flat and need air. If you're a nail spa worker, assigned to poke your fingers through the gaps in multiple peoples' warped toes all day long, your sunny disposition may set rather quickly too. People look down at their feet and they're like "holy shit, who's taking care of these hooves?" The answer is usually you!

When summer comes, the toes come out of hibernation. The heels need to be loofahed and sanded. The toes need to be cleansed, buffed and painted to a dazzling gleam. They're going to be in sandals and popping out of open-toed shoes. Hunks of sock lint growing out of the nails is not socially acceptable anymore. Even men need to step up the game. They're forced to lop the yellow tops off their nails that look like curling, well-tread boardwalk planks.

THE DEATH OF OUR DREAMS

More men are wearing nail polish these days. I have no problem with it. It's not a metrosexual thing -- it's just a thing. Men have every right to be as fabulous as their lady friends. The lines of sexuality are being crossed. Whatever makes you feel good, go for it. In 1955 if you were a man who wore nail polish, you were called 'twinkle toes.' Now if you wear nail polish, people may ask you to twinkle your toes so they can catch the color in a proper light and ask for a color recommendation.

If a man asks me which color I like more for his toe-nail polish, I'll tell him "the middle one." It looks fabulous with their outfit and really brings out the color of their eye shadow.

I HATE
A PARADE

Don't call me un-American. I've shot more guns than the Swiss army. Handguns, rifles... all of them. Crossbows, sling shots and blow guns too. I was in the Cub Scouts, the Boy Scouts, and I almost joined the Army as an Airborne Ranger. I've said the pledge of allegiance a few thousand times and I've saluted more flags than a combat general. I've eaten truckloads of meatloaf and mashed potatoes, and been at the table for every Thanksgiving. If you need me to go down on a bald eagle, I will. I love it here in the good ol' US of A. It's a place I was born and perhaps, if I'm lucky, I'll die here too. Under the conditions of old age and not because some red commie sonavabitch dropped a big nuclear bomb on my head.

But I will be perfectly frank. I hate parades. Can't stand them. Not only do I not enjoy them, I don't understand the point of them. If I wanted to listen to 40 fire trucks blare their horns till my eardrums bled, I'd light a building on fire. Then I could stand there all day and night and listen to the shrill, eardrum-pounding wail those obnoxious red trucks make... most likely, while being blinded by their eye-shattering red, white and blue lights.

Parades have been going on for thousands of years. We use them to celebrate leaders, celebrate war victories, celebrate holidays and celebrate... everything, it seems. Back in the early days of America, when we were in just about every conflict that formed this great nation of ours, we'd pound drums and stomp up every avenue we could find. Main Street USA is the place to be! We get out the auxiliary groups, and the veterans, and the cub scouts, and whatever groups form the foundation of a helpful and sturdy local society. Probably the chamber of commerce as well... and march them around like combat soldiers.

They'll hold banners and flags... the high school will blare their horns and beat their drums. We'll celebrate homecoming, or people leaving. We'll champion immigrants and those who've died. And it's all fine, but I don't want any part of it. The St. Patrick's Day parade is all good. I enjoyed it once long ago. But there's only so many times I can watch 9 different groups of bagpipers march by while they're high-stepping over puddles of green vomit. Usually after the bagpipers pipe-on by, I'm subjected to the firetruck sirens. For some reason, they come by in never-ending convoys. They consist of the fire department from the town I live in, the next town over... and the town next to that. What if a flippin' fire breaks out? Is anyone left to monitor the firehouse?

I suppose the risk of a fire starting is low because everyone is at the parade. I'm not sure why. I can never see anything. I stand behind a packed mob that's ten people deep. I can't ram my way to the front because I'll be standing in front of a pack of four-year-olds waving tiny flags and surely, they deserve to find out how disappointing parades are all on their own. If I try and wrangle my way halfway into the mob, then I'm stuck when I inevitably get claustrophobic and need to hit the nearest bar. If I stand in the back, I'm basically standing next to my town's shoe store that I see ALL the time. I'm completely blind to what's happening back there and then I'm simply *listening* to the parade. I can stand next to the shoe store any day of the week! I don't need a parade to do that. I can summon the sounds of fire trucks on my phone and listen to them wail while I stand outside the shoe store on a Wednesday morning with no parade in sight.

Whenever I go to a parade, I usually bail after about 5 minutes. I hit the nearest pub, but the bars are usually jammed. I squeeze in there and try and get a beer, but there's one bartender for every 80 customers. By the time I get a drink, I want to go home. The roar of the bar makes it impossible to hear. I like quiet bars where I can contemplate life and my inevitable death. No one I know is there because I've failed to make a proper meeting spot with my friends. Even if I wanted to hook up with them, it'd be nearly impossible to connect as the streets and the bars are packed shoulder-to-shoulder with human beings.

The only reason to go to a parade is to get lousy drunk, which is a philosophy I'm totally OK with, except everyone has the same idea. Most parades happen at one or two in the afternoon and by that time, half the town is shit-faced drunk.

Again, that's totally fine by my standards except that once the townsfolk get absurdly drunk, they refuse to move on. It'd be nice if they did move on so I could get zombie drunk and forget that I was at a parade and not doing something more useful like creating art or doing my taxes.

If you have kids and they're in the parade, that's as American as apple pie. Actually now that we're on that subject... I prefer blueberry pie; so apple pie is not my cup of tea. Nor is tea, but that's another subject altogether. I like coffee, which I'll drink by the gallons after I've consumed my five beers at the bar to forget I was at the parade.

Anyway, if your kid is blowing through a trumpet or banging some kind of percussion instrument, then by all means, go to a parade. You should be proud. Hopefully your child won't stop in the middle of the parade and say "Why am I marching down the street with an instrument?" it's an existential question. Why do we do anything? But especially march down Main Street making a shit-load of noise.

I'm the asshole who complains that the parade is blocking all the traffic. I forget there's a parade and I go to the deli because I'm desperate to clog my arteries with a bacon egg sandwich, and suddenly there's people milling about in the middle of the street like they're wandering the rolling hills of some renaissance faire. They're casually walking against a green traffic light as I'm screaming at 50 miles an hour towards them in my two-ton vehicle.

I shout, "What the fuck is going on around here!" then slam the brakes. Then I see a few barricades and five police officers talking to each other and I realize it's a horrible, useless parade.

Like the firemen, there's five thousand cops in the street. This is where you get to size up the athletic nature of our police force. You realize quickly that you can outrun 99% of them without breaking a sweat. They're wearing more equipment than a swat team and most of them have the diets of certain farm animals. You see all the cops and wonder who's watching all the banks. I know they can hop in a car and get to a crime scene if they need to, but there's a million people everywhere. Someone could rob a bank... I mean the actual building... with the bricks and the safe and marble columns, and get away before the cops hop in their car and carefully avoid all the children wandering aimlessly in the streets.

If I run into a parade, I have to look at the calendar and find out what the parade could be about. In March it's St. Patrick's, In October it's homecoming... other than that I have no clue. If I don't hear bagpipes I assume some jerk-off made a holiday up and I have to deal with it. Then I can't get an egg sandwich because there's 40 people in the deli buying beer and cigarettes so they can drink in the street like a bunch of hobos.

A parade usually lasts an hour or two, but the ripple effects of a parade last for days. Not only do they block traffic for miles, screw up your driving route and clog up the restaurants in town, but the clean-up lasts forever.

I've seen green and gold glitter fluttering down the street during the Fourth of July parade. The garbage seems to cling to the earth for so very, very long. They have sweepers and cleaners who come around and try and tidy the place, but it doesn't work! Confetti is nature's worst enemy. Every time someone tosses a handful of glittery confetti in the air, two animal species die off, right there. Turtles hold a funeral, and a panda bear scrapes a line into a tree like a prisoner on death row.

My town has a Christmas parade, which was great when my son was five... but even he burned out on it. The last time we went, it was 10 degrees and everyone that was on every float was so drunk, it looked like the residents of an insane asylum wrapped themselves in blinking lights. They were having more fun than we were. That's not how parades are supposed to work! The people on the floats threw candy canes that smashed to the ground into crumply little pieces. By the time we left, we had little cellophane bags of candy cane dust, which we could either throw away or snort. The following year I asked my son if he wanted to go to the Christmas parade and he was like "Naaa, I'm good." Even he's checking out on the process!

Now a lot of places have a gay pride parade. Gay pride parade?! I thought gay people had good taste! What the actual fuck? I haven't been this disappointed in homosexuals since it was suggested chiffon might pair nicely with acid washed jeans on an episode of *Queer Eye For The Straight Guy*.

One thing I hate about parades is the amount of people *in* the parade. Sometimes the people of prestige are obvious. They have top hats, or canes. They're wearing sashes or holding a banner. They can be well-dressed, in a costume or in a uniform.

But there always seems to be an absurd amount of people marching down the street in everyday clothes. Sometimes they've lost they're group, but sometimes it's huge clusters of people in overcoats and wool hats. They're waving and for some dumb reason we wave back. Who the fuck are these people? If I wanted to see a bunch people dressed in dark overcoats marching down the street, I'll go to the financial district in Manhattan and walk the streets at lunchtime.

Some of them are parents and they're watching over the kids. That's fine. Some are part of a group, and that's fine too. But you can't tell me you've never seen huge swaths of people just matching down the street, uniform-less and completely unattached to any affiliation and said to yourself "Who are these people and why am I waving to them?"

When my son was little, he was in the Cub Scouts and he would be in the parade. So by proxy, I was in the parade as well… which was a small form of torture for me. Then *I* was that plain-clothed dumb-ass waving to people and they were like "Who the hell is that guy?" At one point I left the parade, got a hotdog from a vendor, then ran back into the parade march. People waved to me. I'm not sure why. I was 'hot dog guy' and their lives weren't any richer for having seen me marching down the street eating a foot-long wienie.

My wife is Brazilian and they have the biggest parade on planet earth. Carnival. That's when they celebrate with floats that cost more than some countries gross national product. Considering that Brazil is a fairly poor country with a high unemployment rate, having the eccentric, elaborate and expensive floats seems counterproductive. Sure, people are starving in the street, but lets drive a three story golden float down the road to show everyone a good time! Regardless of cost, it's still a parade and it's a glittering, throbbing, electric nightmare. I'm complaining about a parade in my town lasting two hours… Carnival goes on for something like five days, which is absolutely mind-numbing. A two-hour parade can screw up traffic for the entire day. Carnival screws up traffic for months.

I love New Orleans. It's one of my favorite places in the world. But you wouldn't catch me dead there at Mardi Gras. Mardi Gras, AKA Fat Tuesday is an extension of the Carnival celebrations. Originally a fun, yet sensible celebration for the Feast of the Epiphany, it's devolved into an absolute shit-fest where every dreg of society stumbles into the French quarter to drink from neon plastic tubes, exchange beads for tit flashings and hurl undigested beer onto each other. How this abortion landed on the steps of one of America's great and mysterious cities is a tragedy we'll never be able to comprehend.

Having lived in New York City for 17 years, I managed to avoid the Macy's Thanksgiving parade like the goddamn plague. Mainly because I was out of town with family, dumping multiple plates of food down my gullet until I was in a coma. I fortunately slept through the parade, which for some reason was on TV. If there's anything worse than being *at* a parade, it's watching one on TV.

One year we took my two-year-old son to watch the giant balloons being inflated for the parade the next day. It was, without any doubt, the dumbest thing I've ever done in my life. My son was bored, I was bored. If there's one thing more boring than watching a parade in person and on TV, it's watching the *preparation* of a parade. What the hell are we doing on this planet? Watching scaffolding being assembled at a construction site would have been more illuminating.

One random Saturday, my wife and I were pushing our son in the stroller through Manhattan and came upon a Czechoslovakian Parade marching down 5th Avenue. We stopped to watch and we were literally the only people watching the parade. Who was the parade for? The parade marchers seemed joyous, but we weren't, as we couldn't cross the road. There's 195 countries on the planet! If we have a parade for each one, we'd need to shut the city down for more than half the freakin' year!

In my opinion, parades are a complete waste of time and resources. We spend a lot of money to shut the town down, move people around. Hire cops and firemen, organizers and cleanup crews. I feel we could spend that money elsewhere... like stocking the soup kitchens or adding books to the library. I'd be more than happy to help them with that. I could lead the cause... collect donations and gather the food or books. We could use the money to buy clothing and cook meals. Get toys for kids and maybe something for the families that are less fortunate. Or perhaps we can help unclog the gutters that are filled with confetti, plastic green hats, tiny flags and cheap, cardboard kazoo horns.

Then when the town wants to recognize my efforts, they can give me a citation or perhaps, I don't know, a small party... in a building... or a bar. Hopefully in a bar... that *isn't* crowded with too many people. But most definitely NOT a lousy, time-crushing, ridiculous, noisy parade.

WHITE COLLAR
WORKER

I'm an ordained minister. You don't want me officiating your wedding. I've done two in my life and they both
ended in bitter divorce battles... the kind they make shows
about on Fox with zippy lawyers who frustrate you with their
ability to bounce around the legal system like gymnasts.

One day while minding my own business, my cousin Mary-Lin called me and asked if I wanted to officiate her
wedding. She'd met a great guy and they were going to tie
the knot. What kind of knot I didn't know, but in hindsight,
probably a hangman's noose.

Of course when she called I was a few beers into the
night, so it sounded like the bestest idea in the world! Considering I'd freelanced as an artist my entire adult life; why not
toss weddings into the mix as well? I could roam the country-
side in a converted ice cream truck and stop in small towns,
officiate through the side window and be off before the locals
got too liquored up and rowdy. Easy money.

Mary-Lin did the research and emailed a few links to some churches I could join and be ordained. I clicked and found myself at the portal of *The Church of Spiritual Humanism*. Who they were and what they stood for was unknown. They could have consummated beheadings or championed the raping of children for all I knew, but that wouldn't be any different than the resume of the Catholic Church, so I dove in with both feet.

I don't remember what the requirements to be a minister were, but I don't think it was any more sophisticated than having a pulse, which was a box I could definitely check.

Within days I had some paperwork delivered and my name emblazoned on a card. The card was even laminated, which is more official than you think. Once something of this nature is slabbed in a coating of plastic, it might as well have been blessed by the pope. Most holy men spend years studying the science of theology and deep religious history, but in just a few mouse clicks, I ascertained a community stature the envy of anyone within the sound of my preaching voice.

Before I could officiate this union of forever love, my friends Courtney and Chris caught wind that I was now in the wedding biz and thought it would be a fabulous idea to officiate their wedding as well. Courtney was my ex-girlfriend, so this seemed like a terrible idea, but I was good friends with her fiancé Chris... so it kind of balanced out the weirdness. Chris and I would party and do lots of drugs together, which now made it weird again. But we all decided that this would be a fantastic idea. I'm not sure why.

To convince me this would be an absolute marriage made in heaven – I mean the marriage of me doing their ceremony and not them getting married – Courtney and Chris invited me over to their house for dinner. When I arrived at the door, they weren't home. I rang the bell a few times and as I was about to leave, they wheeled their giant SUV into the driveway and ran out with bags of groceries.

As I drank a beer at the table, they dashed around the kitchen, cooking in a delirious frenzy. Through the madness, they admitted the reason they were late was because they'd been out to dinner.

"So you're having another dinner?" I asked confused.

No, they were making a giant steak dinner -- just for me. A massive side of beef that was accompanied by a dry baked potato and some veggies. The three of us sat around the table and the happy couple watched me choke down a steak while they convinced me to officiate their wedding, which I believe I had already agreed to do.

Of the wedding's many perks was the fact they were throwing a Brinks truck of money at the shindig.

"You'll want nothing" Chris assured me after presenting the idea of every kind of bar imaginable… burger bar, seafood bar, candy bar, and of course, an alcohol bar the envy of all the swanky clubs in Miami Beach. But for every plus, there was a minus. The wedding was in Bal Harbor, Florida, which is gorgeous… but, the price for a room at the Bal Harbor Inn was the kind of money most people spend on their yearly mortgage. The resort was stunning… but, it was taking place in the middle of summer. Summer in Florida is similar to the jungles of Malaysia. The second you step off the plane, your scrotum, tits, and ass stick to other body parts like oily glue. And finally, high ranking on the positive/negative ratio, I'd be at the center of the fun and lavish wedding... but marrying two friends, one of which I'd slept with in the past.

Being the humble holy man I was, my empty coffers couldn't afford me the Bal Harbor inn, so I was forced to reside in the cheaper alternative down Collins Avenue. That place, whose name escapes me, was some kind of rock & roll themed hotel that was really a glorified motel -- its decor not much more than a 1950's high school sock-hop. It was a downgrade for sure, but the advantage was that most of the wedding people needed to stay there and it was right on the beach, so it worked out wonderfully.

After baking in the sun all day and swimming in the clear surf, I did what most men of the cloth do before a bachelor party -- drank heavily. Eventually, the men all piled into a ridiculously long stretch limo and hit the famous Ocean Drive.

With its neon glowing art deco signs and buzzing streets filled with half-naked people, Ocean Drive is the ultimate sea-side siren... luring it's clueless and morally stupid sailors into its den of debauchery. We floated our limo to all the hot spots... green jungle bars where we shouted over the music and passed cocaine under the tables... discos with rotating patterned floor lights that destabilized our shaky footing... and outdoor seating spots that only served as an arena to yell at other, drunker bachelor and bachelorette parties.

At some point we ran into the former mayor of Miami Beach, who, over shots of tequila, kindly recommended his favorite strip club.

Set among what appeared to be the industrial section of Miami, the club was guarded by towering, dark-suited men, who usually flank important leaders of third-world countries. Before we could even worry about entrance, the former mayor magically appeared at our side, where his face alone gained our entire crew entrance without a problem.

The club was straight out of a prince video. A massive black cube, highlighted by purple neon strips and glowing table lights that shadowed the clientele, but not the bare-skinned beauties strutting the place like panthers on the prowl. It's the kind of place Tony Montana would love to be mowed down in a hail of gunfire. Our man of the hour got a lap dance with a six-foot Amazonian and I got acquainted with a Cuban firecracker who... well, let's just say, we were praying on our knees calling to god.

Being the holy man that I am, that's the kind of thing you leave in the confessional.

The wedding went off without a hitch. The ceremony was performed on the beach, under an overcast sky, with a breeze that helped alleviate some of the humidity's debilitating hold. I read famous quotes about love that I gleaned from the internet, and knowing how dependable the internet is, the quote I read about love from Gandhi could have come from the mouth of anyone from Fran Dresher, who played America's sweetheart Jewish nanny on *The Nanny*, to King Leopold II of Belgium, a man who exterminated 8,000,000 people.

Half the groomsmen looked green after all the drinking, tight-necked tuxedos and humid beachy seafood cocktails. Someone even hurled on the sand at one point and went right back to the bar for more. There was enough food to feed an army and although Chris said I would want for nothing, my only want was to give some of the food away as it could have fed half of Dade County and probably everyone on every Key Island.

Courtney was already pregnant, which she'd confessed to not long before, so she spent half the night cleaning up after everyone in her mothering, nesting phase. While picking up chair cushions that had tumbled astray, I told Courtney from the Jacuzzi that she didn't need to clean... that there was hired help to straighten up the mess. Our childhood friend Trish tipped my cocktail to my face and told me not to bother...

"It was something she needs to do."

I left Miami sunburned and cleansed. I drove to Fort Lauderdale and visited my grandparents before heading back to New York where I'd continue my life as a regular old civilian, free from the responsibility of being God's radio to those who might lend me their ear.

Unfortunately, this union did not bind like I'd hoped. There are many reasons that marriages fall apart. Infidelity, philosophical differences... money. I'm not sure the exact reasons but Chris and Courtney divorced.

Chris had some drug issues and needed to go to rehab, but that was not the only reason for the divorce. Usually going to rehab can solidify a marriage. The partner is there to be the foundation for the other. In sickness and in health and in rehab and till death do us part... and all that. But their issues ran deeper.

Strike one for me.

•••

It was the year of weddings for me. It would be three in total. My friends Ned and Jen were getting hitched and they wanted to weave me in somehow. Fortunately I hadn't slept with either of them or anyone in the wedding procession, so the level of awkwardness dropped considerably.

Also of good fortune was the fact I wasn't officiating this wedding. That was left in the capable hands of someone who actually believes in God. Not that I don't believe in God. I do. I just prefer to look at God in my own vision. The last thing I actually worshipped was a wooden head called Jobu that my buddy Kevin and I kept in our kitchen, which we made daily sacrifices to each day. Not bloodletting sacrifices or anything like that... just the occasional coin, button or cigarette, which we offered into Jobu's wooden bowl as a token of our love and appreciation. It was good karma and Jobu watched over us.

Ned and Jen wanted to incorporate their friends and family into their special event -- having them speak at various intervals of the process. I suppose they'd heard me spin a few wild yarns and thought having me yak-it-up in front of their friends and family was a good idea.

Ned asked me to speak at the actual wedding ceremony.

"Sure!" I said enthusiastically, "how about I do famous quotes about love from famous people?!"

Ned was like, 'nah, that's a stupid idea,' and immediately relegated me and my speech to the rehearsal dinner. In hindsight, that was probably best. A wedding ceremony should have gravity and grace. Your stumbling buddies with questionable morals shouldn't be slinging their shit in front of nicely dressed people who traveled far to see a proper union.

Ned and Jen were getting married in Napa Valley, one of the loveliest places in the world. Destination weddings can be tricky. Miami in the middle of summer? Questionable. Wedding in a different country where people need passports and shots? You're asking for trouble. Napa Valley? Yes, please! Oh, man. It's such a beautiful place. And I wasn't even a wine drinker back then. I was a wine drinker after I left!

The whole place is glorious. There's very few places in the world where you instantaneously feel at home... at least for me. Napa Valley is one. The rolling green hills, peppered with large trees... the fertile, yet sandy soils with row upon stunning row of dangling grape fruit ready to be mashed into the velvety liquid gold that has been sipped by everyone from ancient Mesopotamians, to Jesus Christ himself. The air has a special feeling and it's easy to fall in love.

Catalina and I flew into Oakland International airport and stayed in a hotel right on the water. We had a great view of San Francisco and the endless towering robotic steel girder beasts that yank containers from ships in the Oakland Port system.

We spent one day in 'Frisco, dodging the homeless and hitting the sights. Mark Twain once proclaimed *the coldest winter I ever spent was a summer in San Francisco* and I knew that day exactly what he meant. We spent the day climbing the bulbous hills and darkened valley of the city and as the hour passed 3:00 in the afternoon; the city went from a balmy

75 to a frigid 50 in about three minutes. We retreated to a bar to stiffen our resolve with cocktails, but when we ventured outside again, the sky was grey and every person in the street was dressed like they were about to yank outrigger nets full of cod onto the decks of Gorton's fishing trawlers. We wrapped our arms around each other, quick-stepped it to the ferry and made it back to our hotel before hypothermia set in.

The next day, our friends Dylan and Tanya scooped us up in their rented mustang convertible and zoomed us up to Napa Valley. The air was fresh and clean and the wine poured like... well, wine actually. We all hunkered down in our Bed and Breakfast spots and toured the Calistoga area. We visited Francis Ford Coppola's vineyard, which was lovely. I was totally expecting to arrive to see a fully functioning film set, with Francis whirling high above the crowd on a crane, barking through an old-fashioned cone bull-horn, directing his next operatic masterpiece as countless extras stormed over hills with guns and bayonets.

Little did I realize this was a historic, yet simple vineyard and Francis was off doing something completely unrelated to film. Or wine apparently. But we took a tour and enjoyed the wine.

Early the next day, the entire wedding party went whitewater canoeing. If you're going to have a wedding, there's no better way to bond than to get everyone drunk and on a river. Our heads turned beat red from the glistening sun, and every delicate manicure was scraped off every fingernail in the never-ending wash and rinse cycle of the Napa Valley River.

For some reason, our entire canoe-trip crew was high-jacked by a different river canoeing touring company and diverted to some creepy inlet, where we stood confused about where we were.

Apparently, we were in the middle of a river canoeing turf war and it was hardcore. The cruel and conniving psychological game these canoe touring companies play with one another run deep, and we were the innocent pawns in the chess match. After we spent half an hour in a gully, someone alerted us that we'd essentially been shanghaied, and needed to get the bride and groom to the rehearsal dinner quick. Someone darted off, got the car and before we knew it, Ned and Jen were safely whisked away.

Not only did we have to deal with the indignation of roughed palms, ruined nail polish and pruny fingers, we found ourselves knee deep in a river battle, the likes of which were potentially more dangerous than the Crips & Bloods, the Hatfields & McCoys and Martha Stewart & Gwenyth Paltrow.

Eventually we all got back to our hotels and dressed. I gave a rousing speech... I'm sure. I think. To be honest, I don't remember what I said. Something about not telling filthy stories and that I would tell filthy stories at the bar later if anyone was interested. Everything after Coppola's vineyard is a scramble of memories and random images.

The wedding took place in a canopy of trees in a natural open arena. A brass band led the newly married couple to the reception and we enjoyed a wonderful night of celebration.

Fortunately for Ned and Jen, I did not officiate this wedding, so they are still together. I probably shouldn't take credit for their longevity, as they are people with brains and empathy and communication skills. Things that make marriages work.

Completely arbitrary mystical hexes that I may imbue with my God-given powers of the clergy shouldn't really factor in… but you can't completely rule it out.

•••

I was harkened back into the Lord's work on the cusp of early fall. This time, in the easier to digest climate of Maryland, where my services were utilized for the people who'd commissioned me in the first place. My cousin, Mary-Lin and her fiancé Fred.

This was a family thing. Tame in comparison to the Miami heat adventures or even the west coast stylings on Northern California. I was there with my parents, sister and nieces… as well as small children who knew me. Being on my best behavior was encouraged.

There were no raging bachelor parties, no white water shenanigans, no drugs… but there was plenty of drinking. My family drinks. We drink well. We drink hearty. We're not alcoholics, but… well, there's a few alcoholics. Some recovered, some not. I'm German/Irish. Beer is basically a food group to me. I'm not presenting this information as drunken pride. It's just fact.

I'd definitely never slept with anyone at the wedding, so I was good from top to bottom on that front. I know in some states it's encouraged, and even celebrated to sleep with your relatives. But my family is not that kind of family. We reserve the outfit of overalls to garden work and have mostly all of our teeth. We don't need to date someone in our gene pool, as we tend to get out and mingle with other tribes.

I don't remember much about the wedding itself. As I've stated before I have a fairly bad memory. My memory is not hazy from drinking, but just hazy in general. I'm sure the drinking doesn't help, but I can't blame everything on drinking. I blame some of it on my stupid, mushy brain, which had memory issues long before alcohol came into play.

How I'm able to write books, I'm not sure, but my memory comes in intense, vivid chunks, so I need to get up at 3:00am to write stuff down so I don't forget because sure as the sun will rise, I'll wake up with no memory of what I was thinking, and it will be lost forever. It's also the reason I haven't slept in a decade. Having children will do that too, but I'm the type of person who drags their ass around most of the day in a haze and as soon as my head hits the pillow, I have flash memories as clear as a television screen... like about the time when I was eight and I sliced my thumb open on Christmas Eve because I was whittling a stick in my room, so I crazy-glued my thumb closed because I didn't want to fuck up my Christmas morning and spend it in the emergency room.

Anyway. The wedding took place in a restaurant, if I remember correctly. In the glass atrium portion of the place. Sun was shining upon us... God frowning down on me. Because of legal precedent, I needed to have a licensed wedding official to actually be present and say union words, so Mary-

Lin and Fred were actually married outside, b*efore* the ceremony, and what I did was some ridiculous farce that was more like a tap dance number. I was more a witness to the union, so my power of God was snatched right out of my hands as my palms faced the sky in naked truth.

But later, I whipped out my book of famous love quotes and stated a few... which again, could have been said by anyone from Kermit the Frog to Ghengis Khan. By that point the whole love quote thing seemed hackneyed. But it was fresh for this crowd.

Somehow, I was even more nervous because in Florida, I was making a fool of myself in front of a giant crowd of strangers. Here in Maryland, I was making a fool of myself in front of everyone I knew. But the bride and groom kissed, and thanked me, and everyone rejoiced.

The ceremony was great and we all drank into the night. Eventually I was back in New York, doing the work of an artist and not any kind of false prophet, like so many madmen of the street... holding large signs above their heads and shouting "The End is Nigh" and "Drop pants, not bombs."

Unfortunately, this union didn't work out either. There was a whole host of issues with this marriage, but I won't get into it. It's not my story to tell.

Strike two.

There's a good chance there won't be a strike three. My days of freelance ministering are probably over. My vision of the mobile ice cream truck has long since been parked. I'm not sure I was even paid for these two wedding events. If I was, I should probably return the money. If I wasn't paid… shame on them! How dare they take advantage of a humble man of the cloth.

I tossed my Church of Spiritual Humanism card into a junk drawer with a bunch of batteries, rubber bands and pencils. The edges have curled and discolored. It's so warped it probably wouldn't even fit into my wallet anyway. That's a sign from God not to play the game anymore.

The Devil works in mysterious ways, but when the edges of your laminated minister card crust and harden like a razor that will slice you… that's the Lord giving you a clear indication to pack up your collar and get the frock out of town.

THE BAUBLE GAUNTLET

Do you have a Home Goods or a Marshalls near you? I live on Long Island and they're everywhere. These places sell home items like kitchen supplies and clothes that weren't good enough to sell in a regular store. You peruse the shelves and say, "Wow, I can't believe how cheap this non-stick frying pan is." So, you buy it, take it home and everything you cook sticks to it, and you say, "Wow, this is a piece of shit, no wonder no one bought it."

But there are gems to be found in places like this. Shirts, gift items and other treasures... if you dig deep enough. One time I found a great beach shirt with little palm trees on it and I wore the shirt till it practically turned to dust and blew off my body in a strong breeze -- like tissue paper. My wife hated that shirt. That's why it probably lasted so long. It fought against her. She tried to over-wash it and dry it on high heat so it would disintegrate, but it was too much for her. It won.

But one thing I hate about these places is The Bauble Gauntlet. That's the never-ending check-out aisle with row upon row of trinket shit -- cookies, notepads, pens, toys, organizers and just about everything on the planet that fits in your fist. It's an impulse buying nightmare. It's where the worthless shit you didn't buy in the regular aisles goes for one last chance. The kennel of crap. The death row of debris.

Every place seems to have one of these now -- pharmacies, Staples... every place that sells small items. Candy, eyeglass chains, stickers... it just goes on and on and on. Forget about bringing a child into the Bauble Gauntlet! You'll come in for $100 worth of necessities and leave with $800 worth of garbage. These Bauble Gauntlets are freakin' long too. Like 80 feet. Sometimes they have a corner, so not only are you going down an entire lane of knick knacks, but then you have to round a bend and go down *another* row. It's like Lombard Street in San Francisco -- the famous winding road you see in the movies. Only it's packed with yard sale items of people's filthy, worthless shit.

These stores make it appealing to the impulse shopper. It's all the stuff that seems like a wonderful idea on paper, but in reality, is truly horrible. Chocolate-covered chocolate chip cookies are amazing when you're on line and it's lunchtime, but by day three on your kitchen counter, you realize that you might have diabetes.

They sell so many varieties of water bottles you'd think everyone was on a walkabout in the Sahara desert. You snatch one of these bottles off the shelf and it seems state-of-the-art and has metal and glass and can retain the temperature of the liquid of your choice for hours. Then you get home, open your cabinet and stick it with the other 27 bottles you already have.

The Bauble Gauntlet is the ultimate test of want and need. Yes, I know you WANT the mug with three handles shaped like musical notes, but do we NEED a mug with three handles shaped like musical notes? Have you thought about how long those musical notes will last? I see one breaking off after the second wash.

I have to be a negotiator when I'm in the Bauble Gauntlet. My wife and son yank stuff off the shelf and coo with delight. Look! It's a sloth that holds your computer mouse! I cringe… does my computer mouse need a holding station? I think it's fine lying right on the desk. Maybe we can use that $16.95 to buy a couple of egg sandwiches or a smoothie or two. We do need to eat, after all.

If I get out of the Bauble Gauntlet without a purchase, I feel a tremendous sense of relief. Almost like I escaped a torture chamber. But eventually I'll need to go to other stores and they'll have Bauble Gauntlets too. If I can get through three or four of these booby trap nightmares in a row, I call it one heck of a day.

I don't think Indiana Jones went through so many trap tunnels in all his rip-snorting adventures. He had to use physical cunning and history's mysteries to solve complex puzzles to navigate deadly cavern mazes. I need to do the same.

Someone picks up a bag of caramel popcorn and I snap into action. I grab the bag and say something like "This company murders white rhinos" and I stuff it back on the shelf. Suddenly my knowledge of the world's corporations rises to razor sharp levels. I'll even bust out a complaint about

GMOs or rainforest killers. Minutes before I walked in the door I couldn't be concerned with any of that crap, but suddenly my wallet is being threatened and I turn into Jane Goodall. I produce a power point presentation insightful enough to show the EPA's executive board about pollution and carbon footprints and I get it relating back to the fuzzy slippers my wife is holding.

One time my wife bought a hand cream that smelled like a French whore fell into a vat of old rubber. She used it once and I couldn't go near her. When she purchased it, she was elated -- but 3 hours later when the new purchase glow wore off, we were left with an ointment that someone probably rubbed on their dirty armpits during the French Revolution. Completely and totally worthless.

A deal isn't a deal if it's completely worthless. We have a house filled with stuff we don't use. I spend half my time doing hard negotiations in the store. I'm like a reverse salesman. I'm trying to get things flying *ON* the shelf. It's a full time job. I prefer to shop alone because I can be out and home in about 20 minutes -- having only purchased what I needed and hopefully at a fair price. If I go out with my family, I'll be sure to either have an armful of garbage, or disgruntled passengers who wanted a mini watering can or some curio with a third-rate Star Wars character who barely had any screen time in the prequels.

It's like a hostage negotiation in the Bauble Gauntlet.

"Put down the $40 dollar face cream where the seal has appeared to have been broken and I promise you can have that bracelet we saw at the craft fair."

The Bauble Gauntlet has so many things that are appealing on the surface, but worthless at its heart. Those little wooden signs for example. They're grey, and weather-worn... even though they just came from the factory, and have swirly hand-painted messages like "A house is not a home without family" and "Come in and get drunk." These signs are nailed to the wall of every beach rental from Myrtle Beach, North Carolina to the shores of Laguna Beach, California. They come in every shape and size imaginable. I take one look and say "I could make this in five minutes" and never do because I don't want one. My wife holds these and melts as if Mahatma Gandhi himself handed her a personalized message of sage advice. Yes, I realize "Kitchens bring families together" that's because it's where we keep the food.

My local CVS has a Bauble Gauntlet that branches into two separate Bauble Gauntlets. One so you can take your worthless crap to the checkout person -- the other so you can check out the worthless crap yourself.

Self-checkout is the seventh level of hell. The second I start scanning, something goes wrong and I'm forced to ask the attendant for help. The giant light above the computer system blinks and shouts, "Please wait for help!" The CVS counter person has to first complete the checkout process of all the people that were in line behind me, then come over and help me. Sometimes they'll grab my Gauntlet stuff and scan it for me like I'm an idiot; like somehow, I broke the system with my terrible scanning technique.

Christmastime is the worst. The Gauntlet is a gift givers paradise. My wife adds five more people to her gift list and I remove five more years from my retirement fund. Suddenly, we're holding gift items for the school crossing guard or the guy who poured us a coffee at the local deli one day. This place is a store, not Santa's personal Amazon warehouse. I can't gift the entire town. This isn't *It's A Wonderful Life...* this is regular life!

Even I get tempted by the Bauble Gauntlet and I'm supposed to be the reasonable one. I go to buy tissues or headache medicine and I'm in the Gauntlet... it's temptations dancing before me. Bags of sea salt caramel chocolates, hunks of gooey marshmallow things... all calling me with their terrible, overpriced deliciousness. Even worse is when it's 50% off because the holiday it's packaged in has passed us by. Damn you half price chocolate!

That's the worst part of the Gauntlet. Half priced items. My wife sees cut rate Christmas ornaments in January and scoops up a handful or two. They're super cheap! She promises me we won't need to get any more ornaments next Christmas because the massive mounds she's tottering to the register will satiate her lust. I have to shield my eyes from her vicious, scabbard Pinocchio nose because it's thrusting at me like a fencing foil with each heinous lie she tells. They'll have a Bauble Gauntlet at the Christmas store we go to in December and she'll have more handfuls of ornaments then too! We'll need a third Christmas tree to hang all these things on!

We usually buy things like discount ornaments when the Christmas decorations are packed away already. My wife will stuff the new ornaments in my desk drawer and I'll have to look at them every time I go to get a pen. I'll see a cut-rate skiing Santa mouse ornament, glue-gunned together with the skill of a four-year-old and get irrationally angry. These are decorations from a pharmacy… they're pure freakin' garbage! By the time Christmas actually comes the ornaments have been mashed into pieces and have staples stuck in the felt, crumbs imbedded in fabric and tape glued to them. They're now completely and utterly worthless.

That's Bauble Gauntlet purchase regret. I'll take out the crushed ornaments and present them to everyone like I found a dead bird, hoping to implore sadness over our careless purchase history. Unfortunately, this pitiful display usually has the opposite effect. It starts a burning desire to fill the empty hole in their hearts that only buying more crap can satiate. We'll go to the store and buy more stuff. Eventually we'll be in line to buy that stuff… inside the ghastly Bauble Gauntlet… and the process will start all over again.

I'll be swatting away everything from cell phone covers to artisan bags of wagon-wheel pasta and I'll do it with the thinly veiled threat of global warming and terribly overcrowded landfills where tiny, borderline extinct animals are threatened to be buried under never-ending garbage from the Bauble Gauntlet.

NEW YORK
ART SCENE

My first apartment in Manhattan was on a desolate stretch of industrial wasteland called 13th street between 1st Ave and Avenue A. The street didn't have one bit of charm. Not one tree, not one piece of architecture and not one clean spot. It was an eyesore of rusting cages filled with rusting garbage cans, crooked graffiti-tagged doors and piles of trash that doubled as rat habitats. Each dull tenement box was less distinct than the next, separated only by subtle lines of brickwork where buildings slowly melted into the sidewalk at varying rates of decay.

This was before gentrification had fully kicked in. You could still catch glimpses of "real New York" as people from New York liked to say… like drunks getting blowjobs from the homeless and junkies openly shooting heroin on their stoops. Alphabet city was pretty rough even on Avenue A where businesses were operating, but you never really knew what they were selling. Clusters of folks sat on folding chairs along the sidewalk... their arms crossed with Yankee caps yanked over their shaded eyes. They never seemed to work, move, or do much of anything other than smoke cigarettes and listen to small AM radios with high-pitched treble and nary a hint of bass.

I was fortunate enough to secure a cheap ground floor studio flat in the back building of a two-building tenement that once housed the immigrant slaves who built the bridges that line the edges of the island. The front and back buildings were separated by a courtyard with one wispy tree that somehow found a way to grow in a half circle of polluted soil in the urban cement. It produced some leaves and did its part to instill life-giving oxygen to our lungs during the warm months of the year.

My apartment was such a shit-box, only one of the two windows opened and when you turned on the faucet in the dank kitchenette, the lights dimmed. I shared the place with a mouse that would scamper across my back while I slept, and the radiator would blast like a teakettle against the broken window -- steaming it like a carwash.

The place was owned by a slumlord named Steve Harris who, like most slumlords, ran the place like a leper colony. He'd pull up once a month in his beige Lincoln town car, which doubled as his office, and bark orders at Sammy, our one-legged super who also seemed to make only monthly appearances.

Steve would exit his car, leaving the engine running with the door open for extended periods, and brow-beat Sammy into some menial job as fast as a one-legged man could go. Those jobs ranged from bagging the mountains of recyclables that had been sitting for long stretches, to gutting a bathroom down to the studs. Both jobs usually taking the same amount of time and care.

One day, a giant hole collapsed around my toilet, turning any sleepy midnight pee into a game of *The Floor Is Lava*. Sammy remedied the situation by lining rows of duct tape across the hole and painting it with waterproof enamel and calling it a day. I spent the next two years using the toilet, both standing and sitting, at a 90-degree angle. While sitting, I'd rest my arm on the porcelain tank and listen to my neighbors through my small sliding window talk earnestly about who was being eliminated on *Survivor*. When people said they needed to jump in the shower, they said it figuratively... but I would say it literally, or I'd find myself in the basement.

Once a tenant named Molly moved in and thought it'd be nice to plant flowers in the polluted dirt bed next to the wispy tree. Sammy, in his caring sensitivity dumped about 300 pounds of bricks on them before the water she'd sprinkled on them had dried. It was a real Welcome to New York! moment.

The only thing that kept the place from becoming a complete toxic waste sight was Steven's niece Rachel lived in the building. She was a pale-skinned half Jewish girl with a mane of bright, curly red hair. She'd knock on my door every Tuesday night holding a six-pack of Red Stripe beer and before long; we'd be knocking boots on my black faux leather futon.

Our little courtyard did have some allure. The residents would gather to socialize at the wrought iron table with makeshift chairs and sip a drink or two. It was a calm little spot that would catch some rays of sun that poked through the surrounding building's gaps -- a place to get away from the hustle and bustle of the noisy city streets. People came and went from the building like Penn Station at rush hour. The building seemed to house people for only months at a time. New faces were constantly passing through, so the courtyard felt more like a café than a rental building.

One day in 1999, I met a mousy little blond woman from Pittsburgh named Lindsey who stopped to sip some mojitos with me and Will, a pale Floridian who lived on the top floor. At the wrought iron table, she confessed to receiving an art fellowship, so she packed up her stuff and moved to New York so she could create her art at a prestigious Tribeca studio. The art society was paying her rent, studio space and providing her with a stipend to live on. In NYC terms… that was big money. She sounded fascinating and smart; so needless to say, I was dying to see her artwork.

Lindsey was shy about her work, but I figured it was because she was a shy person in general. Some artists are like that. They're scared to share their art because art is a window to the soul, and criticism can cut… sometimes so deep, it can scar the heart. So I could understand her trepidation. She wasn't a total wallflower, but on the subject of her work, she seemed hesitant.

I tried to jostle out of her what kind of art she did, or what her style was, but she seemed to skirt the issue and gave vague descriptions of 'found art' and 'things of that nature.' Of course being an artist myself, my mind ran wild. I imagined tidal waves of garbage art murals running the length of a football field that would render me in awe. I assumed this little mouse was being coy -- that her 90-pound frame was actually welding engine parts together and mounting them to the wall with railroad spikes. Or she was piling mounds of clock parts and coffee cups into thrusting statues of ancient heroes that would confront the viewer face-to-face upon entering her studio.

A few months later, after not seeing her once in that time span -- I assumed she was squirreled away in her studio, creating bit of treasures -- she suddenly appeared and invited me to her first show. She handed me an actual invitation that looked professional and was designed and printed by professional people. It came in an envelope and was accompanied by a small map so I could find her in the maze-like studio agglomeration. She was finally able to show her mid-year work projects along with the rest of the 40 or so artists from around the world in the large Tribeca workspace.

•••

It was a spectacular sunny winter day when I went to the show with Dave, the handsome Mexican who lived in the dank basement apartment across the courtyard from me. He was also invited, so we crossed town to the west side and partook in some alcoholic beverages at a massive glass and wood drinking-hole in the most expensive part of Manhattan. After getting properly lubricated, we headed to the show.

Once inside, we rode a small elevator to the top and were dispensed onto the studio floor. The place was enormous… a massive area that was cut-up into small rooms with drywall. The sun blasted in, illuminating every white room like they were plugged into electric sockets. People milled about in pairs, gently murmuring and discussing what they'd seen... slinking from one room to another.

We poked around and noted nothing of interest. Referencing the small map that accompanied the invite, we tried to locate Lindsey and her inspirational hole. After serpentining around the maze of sectioned cubbies, we found her spot.

Upon entering, I thought we'd entered the wrong place -- perhaps a janitor's room or a place where everyone tossed their trash. But after hearing Dave and I enter, Lindsey rose from a cluster of crap and leaned her smiling face out from a support beam... like a meerkat from a knot of dry grass. She sheepishly tiptoed over -- her hands locked at the base of her pretzel-knotted arms in an 'awe-shucks' kind of way. Without hesitation or chitchat, I went right to the heart of the matter.

"Where's your work." I asked... almost demanding.

The gleam in my eye may have noted the threat of a critic, but I was genuinely curious to see her art and finally drink it in.

She turned and meekly extended her arm as to invite me to look. Dave and I darted our eyes around the place and noticed nothing that seemed remotely like art at all. At least, nothing that we could possibly consider to be art at first glance. But having been an artist my whole life and having seen countless art shows... many of them bizarre and open to interpretation, I opened myself up to her so she could explain her art to me in no uncertain terms.

The first thing she presented was something she had

"just finished" according to her. Untitled, it was an empty, label-less 16 oz plastic Poland Spring water bottle glued to the top backing of a tan wooden chair. The kind of chair you'd see in a school classroom from 1950 through about 1990.

That was it. That was the piece.

The bottle still had droplets of water in it, which made me think this "just finished" piece was just finished minutes before we entered. I tried to show SOME kind of interest in it, but even I, someone who has had a modest amount of amateur training as an actor, could barely contain my WTF facial expression. I kept as stone-faced as I could and turned to Dave, who flashed me his dazzling smile beneath his giant hazel eyes. Dave could grin in any situation and cover the thought he had going on in his mind. His smile did not betray his feelings this time either.

I nodded silently and returned my gaze back to Lindsey, who continued.

Her next "piece" was an empty cardboard six-pack holder of Harp lager, sitting sturdily in the middle of the floor… that was it. That was the piece.

No beer bottles inside the cardboard holder, no droplets of fresh beer still inside the glass. The only distinction it had from garbage was that instead of it being in a garbage can, it was in the middle of the floor… in the middle of the room.

Again, I nodded, only this time a storm cloud grew over me. I'm willing to accept just about anything as art. I understand that we can interpret anything as anything… but this showcase gave me a sense of nihilism I'd not previously known. Perhaps, in her infinite wisdom, that was what Lindsey wanted her art to arouse, although I'd be skeptical of that intention because for every "work" she presented to us, her head descended further down into her shoulders, like she'd been socked by the whack-a-mole mallet of embarrassment. By the time she presented us her final piece, her shoulders were a good inch above the top of her head.

Whether it was her final piece or I was only willing to accept a final piece I can't say. This 'masterwork' was a cardboard box with some papers in it.

Again… that was it. Nothing more, nothing less.

Apparently, these masterpieces are literally everywhere… all over the planet… in every storage closet in every office across the surface of the Earth. Again, I nodded. I'm sure at that point my early bright enthusiasm had dimmed to a dullness not easily sparked again without some kind of chemical or alcoholic fuel.

I'm not, nor have I ever been an art historian, but I believe we'd been down that path before with artists presenting everyday objects as art, which in turn would lead to a debate about what art is… and where the line of art ends and everyday objects begin.

Most famously done by Marcel Duchamp when he placed a urinal on a pedestal and titled it *The Fountain*.

I gave Dave another look, but all he could do was shrug. Even his gleaming smile had gone to a closed-mouth smirk. After a beat or two, Lindsey explained that she entered the fellowship not expecting to win a grant. I'm not sure what her reasoning was, but it seemed that she wasn't really an artist in any way. In some ways, she was apologizing to me for being there and doing this type of thing… although someone on the fellowship committee found merit in her work. Who those morons were, I can't say, but I can only assume they'd just pushed the plunger of some high-grade heroin into their veins when they stamped her approval.

I don't remember what I said after that. I believe in my frustration I politely excused myself and promised to return after we'd seen the other artists. She escorted us to the door and marked that we should check out the girl next door who had these really cool pieces "you'd be sure to love."

Entering that artist's studio, we were met with nothing but an empty room. The only thing of note was that there was a tiny little table in the corner with a laptop on it. We looked around and saw nothing in the bright, white 20 x 20 room.

The girl who belonged to the studio appeared behind us like a ghost and explained that she designed geometric shapes on her computer. She then pointed to her work on the wall. It was one single piece of copy paper with some black lines on it.

Again... that was it.

It was so faint that if she hadn't pointed it out, I would have missed it completely. I swiveled my head around to look for other pieces, but that was it... nothing else. One sheet of paper.

The chitchat we threw back and forth was a fraction of what I'd given Lindsey. Dave and I beat it out of there and continued on... room to room, and took in one lifeless and meaningless patch of art after the next.

I know that art can be many things. Not everyone is a painter or a sculptor. Not everyone gashes mounds of paint across a giant canvas like Jackson Pollack or attacks mam-

THE DEATH OF OUR DREAMS

moth sculpting molds like Jeff Koons. But every room we entered presented one underwhelming artist after another... almost none of which needed a large, expensive studio space to create their art. Isn't that what large studio art spaces are for?

One room had a woman knitting giant colorful macramé quilt pieces. Nice stuff, but did she need an art space to do that? She could be doing that in a rocking chair with her five cats. She didn't need a giant art space. She used the space to hang her stuff, but other than that, it didn't look like she spent any time there at all!

As Dave and I traveled through the maze of rooms, we grew more and more despondent until we came to the conclusion that either art was truly dead, or the fellowship committee were a pack of fools that should be taken to the back of the shed and shot.

At the end even Dave's stellar smile became a straight line. His eyebrows bent into agonizing angles above his hazel eyes, which before, were bright and shiny, and now were just brown.

Before we left, we stuck our heads into Lindsey's studio to bid her farewell at the door. We couldn't even bring ourselves to step inside. While making small talk, couples would wander in to view Lindsey's work and leave almost immediately without any engagement. They too thought they were in the garbage room and zipped out as fast as they'd zipped in.

Dave and I went back to the East Village and drank to forget what we had just seen. If art was to evoke feelings... ANY feelings... then what we'd seen had truly done that. If you go to art shows to be bewildered, depressed, confused and displeased, then this show had accomplished that mission completely.

To compensate for my artistic disenchantment, I painted a massive mural on my apartment wall in all black of a koi fish jumping from a pond surrounded by palm fronds. Part t-shirt graphic, part tattoo... this eight-foot by five-foot mural perfectly accompanied the red rug that my sister gave me. When I moved out years later, I was scolded by slumlord Steve because Sammy had to paint over the mural "a half dozen times" and he took that fee out of my security deposit... of course. If Sammy had only used the waterproof paint he lacquered over the bathroom floor duct tape, the job could have been done in one coat.

Not knowing it then, but the art show was the last we'd all see of Lindsey. Previously I'd not seen her around the building because, I thought, she was toiling away in her studio, creating treasures and pouring sweat into her work. Having seen her work, I couldn't tell you why I'd not seen her again. Her work couldn't have taken more than two or three minutes to accomplish -- regardless of how many pieces she wanted to make. That gave her ample time to do just about anything an artist with a free ride could do... surf the subways, go to peep shows... weave herself into tapestries of human flesh bacchanals. The possibilities of NYC were endless. But when I asked Anthony who lived below Lindsey where she went, I was told "back to Pittsburgh," and that was that.

For all I know, she could be creating masterworks of art that hang in the finest museums of the world, or perhaps, are openly displayed on the floors of the most illustrious art galleries. Maybe she has sold a plastic yolk that once joined a cluster of Budweiser cans for the price one might pay for an actual brewery.

Or maybe her 'plastic bottle on chair' is in the collection of some billionaire that treasures it for all it's worth. I'm not sure if the water droplets made the chair more valuable, but I can only assume the droplets have long since evaporated, changing not only the piece's value, but the meaning of the piece entirely.

And if you are willing to change your mindset, the cardboard box in your office closet that is overflowing with computer keyboards and wires, can be interpreted as an art piece about human nature's unending desire for growth in an unsustainable world that is choking on the cables of our own production.

For me, an empty cardboard six-pack of beer in the middle of the room can only mean one thing... my inherent desire to go to the store and buy more life-affirming beer so that I may fill my veins with the sweet nectar of barley and fermented hops.

THE GOODALLS

Mrs. Devlin was the neighborhood witch in 1979. She yelled at anyone that came near her house like a wild banshee. Her tiny yard was a small compound with scraggly trees and wildflowers. Her driveway was gated by a chain-link fence on wheels that rolled to the side when she took the car out. We'd sing, "she's just a devil woman" whenever we passed by, just like the 1976 hit by British singer Cliff Richard. On Halloween nights, her house would be egged mercilessly until it was 50% omelet.

And Mrs. Devlin's springy fence was exactly where we had them on this Halloween night – two kids from another 'hood – dead to rights. With cans of Barbasol shaving cream in hand, me, Brad and Johnny zeroed-in on them hard. The devil woman was nowhere in sight – most likely bunkered in for the night – listening intently for the eggs to stop beating against her walls.

The two boys held their hands up in defense. The

tall one had a can of Noxzema shaving cream, which was laughable. Noxzema was thick and creamy -- excellent for tough beards, but terrible for shaving cream fights. Barbasol was watery, and once the plastic spray caps were melted with lighters and formed with needles to jettison the cream in a stream, we could hit a person from 10 feet with pinpoint accuracy.

The shorter kid flinched and bounced off Mrs. Devlin's fence and returned with his hand up threateningly. What did he have in it? A rock? Mace? We braced ourselves when his palm revealed a... bar of soap. We laughed! Bar of soap? He brought a bar of soap to a shaving cream fight! Within seconds we had the two strangers coated like foamy Michelin Men, and we sent them back from whence they came, smelling like a Sunday afternoon barbershop.

Cutting through Pace's Lot where we played baseball in the summer, we hopped the fence... through the Illmensee's yard... and back to the Hennegan household where we exchanged candy favorites amongst ourselves like gamblers in the night.

I've dressed for Halloween every single year that I can remember. I was C3PO in '77 in a costume my father made by hand with cardboard, plastic tubes and gold spray paint; the Incredible Hulk where I was stuffed with newspapers to the neck in a green sweatshirt; a Ninja with a sword and throwing stars; Indiana Jones... and later in life, Indy's father – Henry Jones from *The Last Crusade*; Axl Rose of Guns 'N Roses where I hand drew every tattoo on my arms with marker, following my roommate's poster as a reference guide; Kurt Cobain with a bloody gunshot wound to the head; Ginger Spice of the Spice Girls where I showed up to a party in a home-made Union Jack mini skirt and I was the only person in costume besides Han solo and Princess Lea; The Scarecrow from *The Wizard of Oz* that was part of a group that won first prize in a contest; Woody from *Toy Story*; Obi-Wan Kenobi… the old "Alex Guinness" version from the original Star Wars trilogy; Shaggy from *Scooby-Doo*; Gandalf the Grey from *The Lord of the Rings*; Star Lord (Chris Pratt) from *The Guardians of the Galaxy*; and Walter White from *Breaking Bad*.

I consider Halloween an essential holiday. As important as any that we have. More important than accumulating ridiculous amounts of candy is the freedom to transform into a completely different persona… at least for one night. Anyone can mine the depths of their fantasies and come up with anything that strikes their fancy. One can dress in thigh-high stockings, wear fire-engine red lipstick, don a cock-piece made of steel spikes, or represent the undead in dripping buckets of blood and no one would, or should, bat an eye.

Returning home all alone that fateful night, I passed Mrs. Devlin's as the collateral damage from our fight was dissipating. The fence, which before was dripping with thick, foamy cream, had evaporated into light wisps of bubbles that clung to the chain links like fading snow. And the egg whites caught glimmers of moonlight as they ran down the witch's slate-blue shingles like a specter's drippy ectoplasm residue.

If Mrs. Devlin was the wicked witch of the neighborhood, then The Goodalls were surely the haunting ghosts.

Residing in a home that made The Munster's abode resemble a spread in *Better Homes and Gardens*, the Goodalls were the Boo Radleys of the 'hood... the mysterious unknowns. The Goodall's house, around the corner from Mrs. Devlin's and a stone's throw away from mine, was a towering, gothic nightmare. The exterior green paint had peeled in dry curls that clung to the raw, bone-gray wood... exposing its decades of neglect. The surrounding, ancient trees fingered crookedly over the house like a canopy of dragon wings... shading it from the sun... and the monstrous, overgrown evergreen bushes in the front – as high as the roofline -- flanked the front door like two swelling bastions of creepy claustrophobia. The lawn grass swayed like wheat, the street-lined hedges were a tangled row of knots, and their open attic window, which was rumored to have been like that "forever," had a thick, gnarly vine growing into it like a serpent perpetually slithering in.

The ghoulish *Addams Family* were at least a part of the neighborhood association... however twisted and dark their personal diversions may have been. And *The Munster's* not only came to the front door, they smashed right through it.

But no one ever saw the Goodalls. Never heard them. Didn't really know if they existed. The only time they seemed to be alive was the incredibly rare instance when their old, rusting, mint-green Studebaker was abruptly absent from their sand-dirt driveway. Their front walk was never clear of snow; the browning leaves were never raked. The chimney never puffed. There was no door light... no side light ... and the windows never hinted so much as a faint, flickering candle. It was as cold and dank as any place represented in any horror movie since Nosferatu hunched across a theater screen.

Of course, the neighborhood kids speculated what had become of the couple over the years, based on rumors passed down from our elders. Mr. Goodall killed Mrs. Goodall years ago and had her rotting body hanging in the basement. Mr. Goodall died in the attic and the window was open to freshen the air of his mummified, decaying corpse. And then there was the most plausible scenario of all... the Goodall's son had axed them to pieces and was living off their pension funds while the elderly couple was iced in a freezer somewhere on the premises.

The tales of their existence grew taller than their overgrown shrubs. What did they look like? Did they even have children? The Goodalls had been in the neighborhood so long, generations of people had come and gone without so much as a glimpse of the shut-ins.

So, when I passed by the Goodall's house that night after leaving the Hennegan's, I was shocked to see the front door open – a warm orange glow emanating from the interior. The Hennegans and I had rounded the neighborhood at least two times that night and their door hadn't been open during those candy loops. The storm door was closed, but it was easy to see inside with two clean glass panels where rusting screens would normally be. I walked past but doubled back for a second look. The interior of the house was quite clear – a front parlor with a wooden side table and lamp, a chair, the hint of a thick staircase newel post to the left, and a picture on the wall. As warm and inviting as anything I'd seen. I saw an older woman walk past in a white blouse and black skirt and she seemed to be catering to someone out of sight to the right. Her helmet of curly, white hair was accompanied by large, square glasses with a chain that went behind her neck. Like Tweety Bird and Sylvester the Cat's Granny owner.

I was feeling bold and without thinking, I marched right up the rickety brick path and knocked on their door. Mrs. Goodall came immediately holding a bag of what appeared to be tubes.

"Trick or Treat," I said quietly,

She cracked the door open, greeted me warmly and held out the bag. I took a tube and placed it in my pillowcase sack.

This particular year I was dressed as a bum. Probably the second year in a row. A bum is a quick outfit to throw together and you can store endless cans of shaving cream in the interior overcoat pockets. Mrs. Goodall nodded and smiled, looking me over like I was wearing the cleverest outfit in the world.

I craned my neck and saw Mr. Goodall in a comfortable chair, watching an old TV set. When Mrs. Goodall saw my interest, she invited me inside. I stepped in and stood, checking the place out. Mr. Goodall was an old, frail, but healthy-looking man in a grey flannel shirt, and he greeted me with a big nod. He had a wispy head of white hair that was slicked back in a dome. I could have easily been him when I turned 180.

"Get the tray," he said.

Mrs. Goodall disappeared into the dark dining room and returned immediately with an old silver tea tray, intricately detailed from a bygone era... probably the civil war.

Strewn across the top were multiple, full-sized candy bars… Snickers, Milky Ways, Three Musketeers and more. I took one and put it in my sack and thanked her.

Mr. Goodall returned his attention to his black and white television to focus on a boxing match that looked as old as the TV itself. I looked around and took it all in. The wallpaper was turn-of-the-century… a beige hue accented by intricate, browning Damask-patterned flowers. The table lamp glowed yellow, which gave a Halloween amber to the place. I turned to leave, but Mrs. Goodall asked me to stay.

"Would you like some cocoa?" she asked innocently.

I told her "no, thank you" because it was late and I needed to get home. She didn't argue.

I stepped outside, turned and waved goodbye. She smiled and waved goodbye in return through the windowed storm door.

Down the street at a safe distance, I took the tube out of the bag, snapped the rubber band off and unrolled it. It was a T-Shirt iron-on of a monster truck, set before a blazing sun. I looked back and nodded, thinking: "freakin' cool Halloween treat."

I was home in seconds. My parents were waiting for me in the kitchen. I immediately showed my father the t-shirt iron-on that I got from the Goodalls.

"The Goodalls?" he said dropping the newspaper in genuine disbelief.

"Yeah!" I said, "I was there just a minute ago."

He eyeballed me with doubt.

"Get out of here." he said, "You serious?"

"Yes, it was my last stop before coming home."

I quickly explained the front door being open... the warm light... and stepping inside. He didn't believe me, but I was adamant. So, he and I decided to head over to the Goodall's to check it out. We were there in 30 seconds.

When we arrived, the place was as dark as ever – black as midnight. Not a single light was on. The front door was closed and there wasn't even a hint of light anywhere to be seen. Not a crack of light under the door... not a window with a glow of orange. My father paced back and forth in the street, like a thief trying to locate an entry point... shrugging at me and shaking his head.

Then, he cautiously crept up the walkway... just as I had boldly done no more than five minutes before. He carefully leaned forward and gave a gentle knock on the door.

Nothing. No answer.

He gave a series of firmer bangs and stepped back.

Dead silence.

I made a final plea that I was "just here, standing inside and speaking with the Goodalls face-to-face." They gave me the iron-on and a full-sized Milky Way bar. But the longer we lingered, the more ominous the place grew. There was absolutely no signs of life and the stillness of the cool Halloween air gave us the chills.

We left and returned home.

I never saw the Goodalls again after that. No matter how many times I rode past on my bike, I never saw their open door again – for any reason. Not for air, not for sunshine... not to get the mail. Not for the fourth of July and not at Christmas. The following Halloween their door was dark and when I passed back and forth a few times on my way

AND OTHER FUNNY STORIES

home from looting the neighborhood of candy, no warm light invited me in. The same went for the next Halloween… and the next one after that.

The more I've thought about that night, the creepier it gets. People love a good ghost story, but I don't believe in ghosts. At least I don't think I believe in ghosts. I don't believe the Goodall's were ghosts, but it's hard to make sense of what happened that night. A one-night appearance? A final Halloween goodbye? I can't say.

We left the neighborhood in the summer of 1984. Over the years, I would drive through to see what changes the 'hood underwent. A woman I took Jiu Jitsu with bought Mrs. Devlin's house and removed the gate. But the Goodall's house remained – completely untouched like it was when I was a kid. Then about a decade ago, I drove through and not only was the Goodall's house gone; a huge, white Craftsman house with black trim and roof had replaced it. The trees were cleared and the house glowed with full exposure to the sun. The opposite of the Goodall's green-hued tomb.

The only thing that remains of the Goodall's memory is the graveyard of dead bodies the new house was built upon.

I'm kidding!

I'm sure they removed the bodies.

THE DEATH OF
OUR DREAMS

It crept up on me slowly. Like a stalker. I was having chest tightness, which was concerning, but nothing I hadn't dealt with in one way or another before. Typical man -- avoid any health signs until it's almost too late. But one night, they were severe, and my arm began to tingle.

I did what any rational and intelligent person would do. I Googled my symptoms. Ding – Heart Attack! I swear on a stack of Bibles I was going to die right then and there. Then it hit me like a like a bomb. A lightning bolt through my core.

I stumbled into the next room with my hand pressed against the wall. Catalina, my live-in girlfriend, took one look at my ashen face and her mouth dropped.

We tossed on our coats and rumbled down the crooked stairs of our apartment building and into the street. The freezing air shot through me, and I shivered uncontrollably. Catalina gasped, "Oh my god" which made the trembling worse. We fell into a cab and went to the nearest hospital... Mount Sinai Beth Israel on the corner of First Avenue and 16th street.

They put me through a battery of tests that included wires, needles, and beeping monitors. Things I loathe. The results were nothing. Just an anxiety attack. Then they handed me the bill. I almost had a REAL heart attack. I didn't have insurance... or any money for that matter. I was unemployed at the time. They wanted to keep me overnight for observation, but all I heard was "We're willing to triple your bill if you stay a few hours longer." So, I left.

At that stage of my life... or as some might say, 'at the crossroads'... one might begin to feel the pull of their existence. They'll reference the crooked directional sign pointing in all directions for help. Some encounter this intersection in a few ways. Some might stamp it a midlife crisis and buy an expensive convertible automobile. Others have been known to discard their whole life and hookup with a lover half their age and travel to exotic locations.

I traveled the road taken by many and had a brutal, debilitating mental breakdown.

Back on the internet, I searched for a doctor, or a therapist... someone to help me. But trying to find mental help when you have no money or insurance is like trying to buy a house with Monopoly Money. People act as if you're completely out of your mind, which on some level you are.

Their faces say, "The gall to be sick and have no money. How dare you!"

But you didn't plan it that way... it just happens. I managed to contact a doctor on the phone and the sympathy in his voice as I pleaded for help was tangible. I could tell the system had worn him down as he sighed because I answered 'no' to all his questions of payment and insurance. I wasn't even in the immediate area to run to him so he could at least see me face-to-face. As I hung up the phone, I could hear the sadness in his voice as he believed he'd "lost another one."

I started work at HBO, which snapped me into a temporary groove because I could afford rent and food, but the effects were short lived. One morning, Mary Tchobojian, the wonderful art director who hired me, rounded the corner and was shocked at my appearance. She was motherly and concerned. I was skinny to begin with, but she remarked on my gaunt, drawn-out nature. My diet consisted of cigarettes and a daily bite of a tea sandwich that I procured at a Japanese café on my street... the only thing I could choke down.

Then, the HBO art department transferred me to another department, and I felt like the rug got pulled from under me. I went from a bright-windowed office to a darkened cave in an adjacent building. The storm cloud hanging over me turned into a tornado.

I was spinning out of control and clinging desperately close to the edge.

I finally called my sister and she spoke to me in a clear and understanding voice. She told me to get help immediately, any way I could... and I did. I went to the health clinic at HBO, and they called a doctor. I went to see a psychiatrist named Dr. Berger or something like that. Honestly, I can't remember him too clearly. He looked like Bill Gates and had the personality of a cardboard box. I started anxiety medication. Hated it. I felt terrible and couldn't get an erection, so I switched to something else that worked on all fronts. Later, I found out it was a powerful medication for schizophrenia and deep psychological issues, so I stopped taking that, cleaned out my system and simply toughed it out.

It was hard. Social acceptance of depression and anxiety is becoming more common, but back then, I felt like I needed to keep it quiet. Anxiety and depression are considered a weakness and it was an incredibly difficult time for me.

"Suck it up, pussy" is a term you can hear rolling in the back of your mind if you dare speak about it in polite company. It's a cultural thing.

When someone breaks their arm, you don't shout at it, "Suck it up pussy. Get back out there and work again!"

You put a cast on it and let it heal. The same goes for a broken psyche. You don't wrap a cast on it... it's much more complicated than that. But you take care of it properly -- with time, therapy, and if needed, some medication. Eventually, it will heal. Hopefully, it will heal.

Mental health can't be cured with a firm knock on the shoulder and a hearty "Get over it" – a philosophy we've been using since the dawn of time. I needed support and I was afraid to find it. I didn't really know WHERE to find it.

It's a spotlight on our terrible and completely broken healthcare system. But what are we to do at this point? Old folks often choose between medicine and food. A trip to the emergency room can cost you thousands; and don't even think about a tragedy or serious illness—something severe could make you poor for the rest of your natural born life.

Cancer or any other big life hurdle can wipe out your finances or put you in debt forever, without any way to climb out of the hole. It's frightening! It makes you think about life differently. One bad step off a curb or one wrong move can cripple you and your bank account for a long, long time.

But it's hard to get mad. What can we do? Picket in front of health care and Big Pharm companies? They're powerful enough to wipe you and your family off the Earth in the blink of an eye. They'll do it overnight when everyone is sleeping or watching *The Bachelor*. Don't think they won't.

I'm not sure how... I suppose after a hunt on the internet yet again, I found a therapist who worked on a sliding scale, which meant I'd be donating to him on the low end of the spectrum. Ari was a calm and kind man, but our sessions seemed forced. They'd start with him staring at me and smiling -- blinking and nodding -- which I believe was an open invitation to start spilling the beans about what was torturing me. But I didn't know what to say.

After a few sessions I just talked about anything, whether it was relevant to my deep psychological issues or not. Mostly I'd just blather on about whom I was sleeping with. Some of the sordid details were so intricate, it came across as bragging. I mean, I had to tell *someone* these juicy stories. Ari seemed just as good as anyone. Maybe he could see everything I couldn't... hence the constant nodding. I looked in the mirror and saw nothing. For Ari, I'd mix in the occasional story about drugs and even a Knicks game or two.

What was there to analyze?

What was the cause of my anxiety? With my own eyes, I watched two airplanes fly into buildings and people fall out of the sky.

Was that it?

I was living in near poverty in one of the most expensive cities in the known universe.

Was that it?

My life looked nothing like the thoughts and dreams I had as a kid... was that it?

How insignificant was I?

How important could I be?

Did I want to be insignificant? Did I need to be important?

What was I doing in my little corner of the world?

Existential questions. Continuously.

Do I matter?

Is my art worthy of attention?

Am I talented?

Am I anything more than a simple drone that buzzes in and out of a meager and pointless existence?

People say you can be anything you want if you work hard enough, but it's not true. Not *really*. I mean let's face it, there's only one spot to be the president of the United States every four years. Sans assassination. Lincoln and Kennedy taking pops to the noodle, and McKinley and Garfield (James A., not the cat) taking lead to the guts may open a spot. Those examples may dissuade you from taking the job in the first place. But the job is not readily available. So, your chances of being USA's Big Cheese Número Uno are slim in a sea of 100,000,000 candidates. Some seemingly glamorous jobs have higher acceptance rates. They seem obtainable... like movie star. But they're almost as slim as president.

NYC is where the unwanted, the misunderstood and the dreamers go to find their people and that's exactly what happened to me.

Not that I was particularly lost, but I didn't know how lost I was till I got there. And like me, you see the eager faces of everyone on the street... some are fresh, some are tired... but everyone is hustling, and they're all dedicated to making the dream come true.

You see black kids on the streets and the subway, rapping and handing out mix tapes trying to be the next big hip hop star. The rhyme-spitters trying to be discovered.

I would always grab one if offered and would listen. Usually they were terrible, but they were out there doing it. Trying to make the dreams come true... or just get away... make a life. Their dreams no different than mine. For every black kid from the Bronx hoping to be the next JZ, there's an equal number of white kids from the 'burbs trying to be the next Scorsese.

Because they believe.

They have hope, and they have talent, and they think they can do it with hard work and hustle.

Passionate dreams are dreams no matter the color of your skin or the occupation you're shooting for. Unfortunately, not everyone makes it, and the world needs ditch diggers and servers and garbage men. Some of those are good jobs. Really good jobs. But no one grows up saying they want to sell office furniture for a living.

They want to go to space or run a country... they want money and respect.

Maybe fame... or health insurance.

Most people are influenced by the heroes they strive to be. For years, I worked for these two guys from the Bronx who wanted to be the next Daymon John of FUBU. They worked hard all day at normal jobs, and at night we'd get together and design their logo, clothing graphics, color swatches and all manner of designs. Sweatshirts, hats, jeans, jean stitch patterns... everything. Daymon John designed his own clothes. He became insanely wealthy from it – turned a dream into a huge business. These two guys from the Bronx wanted that too. That was their hero. John did it the hard way, from the bottom... selling clothing out of the trunk of his car. If he could do it, they could do it. My dream was to make movies. Robert Rodriquez made El Mariachi for $7,000.

If he could do it, I could do it.

But I could never find the way in. Film is a hard nut to

236

crack. If you can play basketball, you pick up a ball and start playing. If you're truly exceptional someone will find you. They always will.

But how do you get found in film? It's not like you're sitting on the bench and the coach calls you in.

"Hey Schmitz, get in there and make a film. Let's see what you got!"

It takes time, resources, dedication, and knowledge. You generate connections and luck and maybe if you're blessed, it all comes together.

But I never found the way and the further I dug into my life, the further the dream faded away. I couldn't find the key that unlocked the relief to my anxiety. All the other questions crept into my life. Who was I? What was I doing with my life? Where am I going?

I sat and blinked at my therapist Ari, and he blinked back.

Then Ari announced he was opening his own practice in Brooklyn and that I could see him there... so I never saw him again. I lived in Manhattan. Anyone who lives in the five boroughs knows you avoid travelling to the other boroughs unless it's absolutely necessary.

I dropped the therapy and did what most people in these situations do -- drank alcohol, did drugs, wandered the streets aimlessly for answers, and stuck my nose in all the wrong places. I was a support system away from living in the park. You can see how easy it is for people to fall through the cracks.

I had family and friends who could be there for me.

There's millions of people who don't have anything at all, and it's a frightening scenario; one in which many people fall prey to -- the silent struggles of mental illness.

They fight with all their might... and many times lose.

I was stressed and the ghost of panic was hovering over my shoulder. I was living with Catalina who I wasn't sure I really liked, let alone wanted to live with. We were eating day-old sandwiches from the café she worked. Rent was scraped together with odd jobs and savings.

I compounded the crazy by sleeping with Valerie, my friend Nancy's best friend. We'd hook up every Saturday morning and go to an Italian restaurant for brunch.

Then Catalina moved out and I started dating Valerie. But then I switched the situation and started screwing Catalina on Saturdays and having brunch with her. I was an absolute mess.

My sister was a tremendous help to me in those dark days. Caroline was always a calming influence in my life. Even as a child. For some reason, everyone always came to her for advice and a shoulder to cry on. It's a job she seemed to embrace early on in life... even when she suffered some of her own demons. For me, she was a beacon of light in a stormy time.

But the one thing that finally got me through that time, no matter how stressed I was, or how terrible my decisions were, was a self-healing realization -- a confrontation actually.

I'm not sure of the exact moment when that realization occurred. I don't believe it was a huge moment. I wasn't shouting at a dragon-shaped cloud as beams of sunlight roared down upon me... it was just a simple moment. A few seconds of internal dialogue. And it was just suddenly there. In milliseconds. An unlocking. I think I was in front of a taco stand in the West village to be honest. I didn't have a near death moment... not a city bus coming at me... not a falling brick crashing near my feet... but it was about death. A confrontation with death.

I looked at death... as
an actuality,
as an inevitability...
as something to be embraced and not feared,
and I accepted it as part of life.
And like a snap of the fingers...
my anxiety washed away.

Truly. It was like that.

I gave myself permission to live. To just live... knowing that death would come, and pain, and hurt... and potentially more anxiety... but to just live. And if you want to live, you must know that death is coming. It's the balance of life.

Hot/cold. Up/down. Life/death. It's that simple.

And that was truly a 'first day of the rest of my life' moment and I've felt completely free and confident from that day forward.

Perhaps, it was a portal to a place where life becomes magical and you appreciate it because it may not last forever and you need to enjoy it to the fullest.

But death comes in many forms -- actual death being the most prominent. The heart stops, the blood no longer flows, and the brain goes blank... as far as I can imagine. But there are deaths that are smaller than actual death, but still scary and painful. Sometimes excruciatingly painful... or perhaps you can say, not as deathly as death itself, but significant in its death just the same -- the death of something or someone else that is not actually you. Those deaths need to be embraced and confronted as well.

The death of your car, the death of a relationship, the death of a pet, the death of a family member, and of course, the death of our dreams.

It's painful, the death of a dream. It hurts. There's a saying, "don't continue to hang on to a mistake because you spent a lot of time working on it." It's apt in this situation. You can hang on to a dream so long that you don't realize it's hurting you. The restaurant you dreamed of opening... you put all your money into it and nurtured it, but it's dying... it's not surviving, so you place the last bit of your life savings into it hoping to keep it alive and before you know it, you have nothing. Not the restaurant, not any money... and certainly not your heart, because it's been ripped from your soul. You start almost from the beginning... like a child... although you're an adult with adult feelings and adult problems. It's incredibly painful to let go of a dream. And when you finally let go after hanging on for so long, it can leave you barren inside.

I lived in a world where I was told any dream can happen.

We tell children the stories of dreams because we don't want them to start off life thinking they can't achieve everything under the stars.

Then you go on telling *yourself* you can achieve everything under the stars.

You take control of the narrative. And dreams can come true. But they can also come crashing down... and when they do... it's a death like any other death.

Maybe, the most painful death of all.

The death of your dreams.

The death of the dream of home ownership... the death of the dream of having children...the death of the dream of having a career you love... of doing something meaningful with life... of making change in the world... or of perfect happiness.

Because when a dream dies, you're left with cold, hard reality.

And when there's lots of time remaining before you *actually* die, you wonder if you'll ever have another dream again... and if there's anything worth living for. When a death occurs, it can leave a hole in the heart that you can genuinely feel – like wind is passing through it. A cavity that is so bare, you fill your lungs to capacity in hopes that the temporary influx of air into the chest cavity, will alleviate the emptiness... so you take the next step.

There are dreams that many consider to be reasonable that become unattainable as you move forward through life. There is a very real chance I will never be a homeowner in my lifetime. The cost of homes, the markets, inflation, and unpredictable income have put this dream almost completely out of reach for me.

The initial ideals of the American Dream were of sharing so that we could lift each other up so we could live comfortably in a society that treasured equality. A place where everyone could ascend, to a certain level of comfort, both economically and socially, and a desire to share this with others.

That will, of course, be misconstrued as Socialism and beaten into submission by the dull billy club of every profit-seeking shark. But now more than ever, it's become a game of who can grab more, regardless of the pain that is left in the wake. The money grabbing, me-first, screw the consequences because "I'll be long gone when it all comes crumbling down" new world order. All the generations that are coming down the pipe will forever be surviving... the word 'flourishing' might be eradicated from their vernacular.

But when everyone is chum and the sharks have had their fill, who's left to grind up? When the banks have bought all the houses and have priced everyone out of them, who are they going to sell them to? Not to me, and probably not to a lot of people I know. So, I've been forced to reevaluate another dream and reform it into something else. Perhaps travelling and having a freer nature than I might have if I were tied down by the constraints of a concrete and wood holding cell called a home.

Unfortunately, once you come to terms with not having a home that is yours, the soul becomes a nomad. A gypsy. You disconnect from people because you don't know when or if you'll be moving on. Your soul wanders aimlessly without a purpose. Your dreams become a wish to find a place to lay your worried head or you'll forever be wandering in your heart and with your feet. Inexplicably, you can also become stuck. Your gypsy soul can't go anywhere because you're tied to a paycheck that trickles in, week after week, and is just enough to keep the pilot light lit, but never enough to fuel the fire.

The dream of making a film that I longed to do since I was a kid is shrinking further and further into the rearview mirror as I drive towards an unknown destination. I'm a storyteller and an entertainer, but I'm driving down a new avenue where I can do that in other ways. Maybe it's through writing books, stories or jotting down ideas in journals that no one will ever see.

The new vision is to raise my son and have him be the best person and the happiest he can be. I will instill value and empathy in him. I will teach him skills and give him ideas that

I learned through trial and error over the course of my life. He can be the better version of me, and I can help him achieve the goals he dreams of accomplishing.

When you reach the crossroads, you must take stock of the pros and cons before moving in a certain direction. You may realize that your dream won't happen, so you take a certain road in which you can help others achieve theirs. You shift from taker to giver. Or if you want to do real comparables... from leech to host. Or student to master. Naïve upstart to wizened sage.

Time moves incredibly fast.

The world's children quickly become the dreams of the future, where we can feed them hope and unite them in as perfect a world as we can. Encourage peace, instill love and binding, universal oneness.

It's the righteous battle cry of every soldier that has died on the battlefields for unification... who've died fighting for love, peace, and equality since the dawn of our time. World peace being the ultimate goal.

Maybe it's time for a new Dream. A new *world* dream. Can I change the narrative of the old one? Perhaps I've got to reconstruct the vision. Instead of a dream job, my dreams stay in my head, and they satisfy me by feeding the depths of my imagination. My hobbies can become my dreams and I practice their art in my free time.

Is it managing expectations or the new world order?

I know we can all start off with the dream of 3 kids, a huge mansion and unending wealth... which can devolve to 2 kids, a small house and meager paycheck... all the way down to a few coins in hand, wondering if that's enough money to get you a double cheeseburger or just the single patty.

But maybe the dreams of our youth are things we cling to and don't realize that our hearts and minds have changed.

We must reconstruct our dreams and see life for meaning way beyond our current existence.

Life is managing the pain of the deaths that surround us.

Especially our dreams.

But the beauty of the human soul is that it can be a dream factory and constantly produce new dreams. Ones that you can fulfill in other satisfying ways.

But first we must confront the deaths... of family, of jobs, of dreams... bury them, and start over.

And then, we may achieve some form of happiness.

Made in United States
North Haven, CT
27 September 2022

24612328R00143